ML
686.3 St34
Stein, Jeannine
Re-bound : creating handmade books

P9-CSE-920

WITHDRAWN

re-bound

creating handmade books from **recycled** and **repurposed** materials

BEVERLY MASSACHUSETTS

QUARRY BOOKS

JEANNINE STEIN

© 2009 by Jeannine Stein

All rights reserved. No part of this book may be reproduced in any form without written permission of the copyright owners. All images in this book have been reproduced with the knowledge and prior consent of the artists concerned, and no responsibility is accepted by the producer, publisher, or printer for any infringement of copyright or otherwise, arising from the contents of this publication. Every effort has been made to ensure that credits accurately comply with information supplied. We apologize for any inaccuracies that may have occurred and will resolve inaccurate or missing information in a subsequent reprinting of the book.

First published in the United States of America by
Quarry Books, a member of
Quayside Publishing Group
100 Cummings Center
Suite 406-L
Beverly, Massachusetts 01915-6101
Telephone: (978) 282-9590
Fax: (978) 283-2742
www.quarrybooks.com

FOND DU LAC PUBLIC LIBRARY

86.3
A34

Library of Congress Cataloging-in-Publication Data
Stein, Jeannine.
  Re-bound : creating handmade books from recycled and repurposed
materials / Jeannine Stein.
     p. cm.
  ISBN-13: 978-1-59253-524-8
  ISBN-10: 1-59253-524-0
  1. Bookbinding—Handbooks, manuals, etc. 2. Books—Format. I. Title.
  Z271.S74 2009
  686.3—dc22

2008052264

ISBN-13: 978-1-59253-524-8
ISBN-10: 1-59253-524-0

10 9 8 7 6 5 4 3 2 1

Design: Kathie Alexander
Cover Design: Rockport Publishers
Photography: Glenn Scott Photography
Illustrations: Lisa Li Hertzi
Technical Editor: Marla Stefanelli

Printed in China

CONTENTS

INTRODUCTION

Making a book is one of the most satisfying artistic pursuits. Books offer limitless possibilities—they can be functional, sculptural, or both. From concept to design to construction, each step offers challenges and opportunities.

Most functional handmade books—journals and photo albums—are made from some combination of book board, paper, bookcloth, and leather. In over a decade of creating books out of these materials, I've never tired of learning new techniques and perfecting old ones.

But book artists are always looking for more. After years of using traditional elements, I found myself inspired by unorthodox items—nineteenth-century photographs, rusty hardware, textiles, roof flashing, and cracker boxes. I was excited at the prospect of working with unconventional materials, and I discovered a different kind of satisfaction in taking an item intended for a specific function and recycling it into a one-of-a-kind book.

A recycled book's theme or function can match the materials—or not. An empty pasta box could house recipes, or bingo cards could become a baby book. There are no rules or limits.

An added bonus to using recycled materials is that it's eco-friendly and keeps trash out of landfills. It also reminds us that although we live in a throwaway culture, things can, and should, be repurposed whenever possible to live another life.

The projects in this book incorporate a wide variety of materials that, while familiar, may not be in every book artist's repertoire. For those who have made books before, I encourage you to embrace potato-chip bags and window screens and take your artistry to a new level.

For those who are venturing into completely new territory, this is a great way to start making books. Materials are as close as your kitchen cabinet, and the basic tools needed are few and inexpensive.

Also use these projects as inspiration for further endeavors. Devise creative challenges with yourself and friends to see what kinds of books can be made from automotive supplies, toys, or old clothes.

So dive in. Any day you can make a book is a good day.

Jeannine Stein

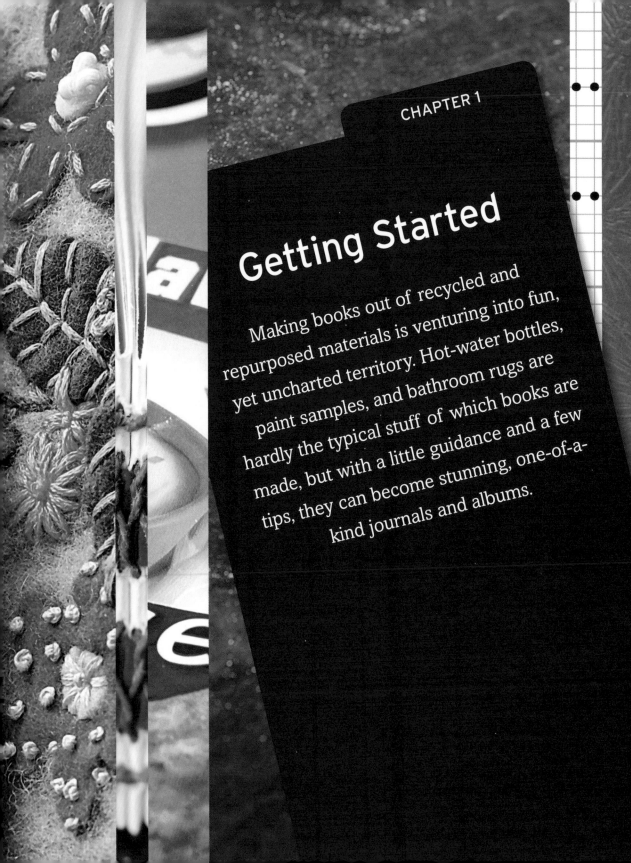

CHAPTER 1

Getting Started

Making books out of recycled and repurposed materials is venturing into fun, yet uncharted territory. Hot-water bottles, paint samples, and bathroom rugs are hardly the typical stuff of which books are made, but with a little guidance and a few tips, they can become stunning, one-of-a-kind journals and albums.

Unfamiliar materials present creative challenges that start ideas flowing. The best way to start working with new supplies is to handle them and see what they can do. Can they flex enough to wrap around a text block? Are they easily cut with a craft or utility knife? Which adhesives work best? Does an object lose or gain appeal if it's pared down? Potato-chip bags, for example, don't suffer at all when cropped, since their bold, iconic images are so easily recognizable. Set aside time to experiment.

Some materials may need shoring up before they reach book status. Extremely lightweight items such as potato-chip bags can be reinforced with Tyvek, a high-density polyethylene that's used for home building and overnight shipping envelopes. Fabric gains heft by fusing it to inter-facing. Even brown paper grocery bags make sturdy linings.

Bindings add another exciting element to books. Most traditional bindings can be applied to recycled items—cabinet cards are made of chipboard, so they can be bound with a simple accordion structure or a link stitch. But don't stop there—recycled items also lend themselves to developing new bindings. Take advantage of elements such as metal mesh and rubber to produce innovative stitching patterns.

Parts of a Book

Bookbinding has its own terminology, and it helps to know the anatomy of a book:

Head: Top of the book

Tail: Bottom of the book

Spine: Edge where signatures are sewn or pages are bound; may be open or closed

Fore edge: Where pages open

Hinge: Material that connects parts of the cover so the book can open

Text block: Inside pages of the book

Folio: Single piece of folded paper

Signature: Several folios nested together. Nesting several folios causes the fore edge to push out; this is called the fore-edge creep, or just creep. The heavier the paper, the bigger the creep will be. The creep can be left as is as a mark of a handmade book, trimmed off with a heavy-duty paper cutter, or removed by holding a metal ruler firmly on top of the signature and slicing off the edges with a craft or utility knife. The creep is important to keep in mind when measuring a book because it will add to the signature's width.

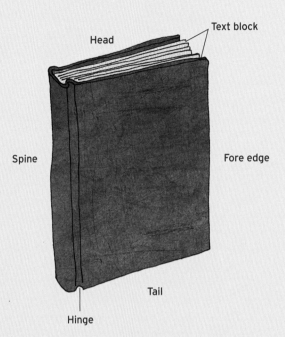

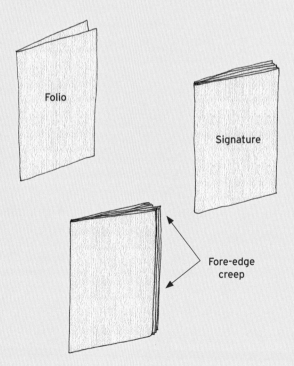

Tools

CUTTING TOOLS

A craft knife is best for making straight, clean cuts on paper and cardstock. Heavier materials require a utility knife, which has a stronger blade, and is best for chipboard, heavier weight book board, and even some lightweight metal. Replace blades at the first sign of dulling.

Scissors are handy for almost every project, and a small pair is perfect for detail work. Teflon-coated scissors are nonstick and good for cutting tape.

Rotary cutters create clean, straight lines on fabric and leather and are used in combination with a quilting ruler and cutting mat. A cutting mat is also essential when trimming with a craft knife or utility blade, since it protects the surface underneath and allows for clean cuts. Cutting paper and cardstock into smaller pieces can be done with a paper trimmer, found at office supply, art, and craft stores. The paper may also be cut by hand, using a craft knife and a metal ruler. To measure the size needed, make two marks at the top and bottom of the paper and line up the metal ruler with the marks, and then cut. Use this hand-cutting method to cut larger pieces of paper that won't fit inside a paper trimmer.

For projects requiring several pieces, label each piece as it is cut by marking lightly with a pencil, or by writing on a piece of repositionable tape and affixing it to the piece.

NEEDLES AND THREAD

Needles made specifically for binding books have slightly blunted points, but darning needles found in fabric stores work just as well. Look for needles with eyes that can accommodate waxed linen thread, but are thin enough to go through small signature holes. Tapestry needles have blunted points and larger eyes that can accommodate wider ribbons and hemp cord.

Waxed linen thread in standard 4-cord size is used for most projects in this book; it's extremely strong and comes in a variety of colors. Other materials suitable for binding include unwaxed linen thread, strong woven ribbon, and hemp cord. Other threads can be used, but test for strength by pulling; if it breaks or stretches, don't use it.

Coat unwaxed threads such as hemp cord with beeswax so they'll slide easily through signatures and covers and to help get the kinks out. Pull thread through the wax two or three times before sewing.

AWLS AND DRILLS

Use awls for punching holes in signatures and covers. Heavy-duty awls, found in hardware stores, can punch larger holes in paper, board, and fabric. Hand drills quickly make uniform and neat holes. Use an "anywhere" punch with a hammer to punch holes in cardstock or heavy book board.

▶ **Top: A**, scissors; **B**, craft knife; **C**, utility knife; **D**, small detail scissors; **E**, nonstick small detail scissors; **F**, rotary cutter; **G**, cutting mat
Bottom left: H, beeswax; **I**, hemp cord; **J**, waxed linen thread in various colors (blue, yellow, red); **K**, tapesty needles; **L**, binding needles; **M**, ribbon. **Bottom right: N**, sturdy awl; **O**, lightweight awl; **P**, rotary hand drill; **Q**, heavy-duty awl; **R**, hammer; **S**, "anywhere" punch.

BONE FOLDER AND ADHESIVES

Bone folders are indispensable tools that make neat, flat creases and smooth paper after gluing. They can be made out of bone or plastic.

PVA, or polyvinyl acetate, is the preferred glue for bookbinding. It's archival, is non-yellowing, and won't crack with age. Archival glue sticks are best for quick, small jobs. Thick craft glue adheres fabric and small dimensional embellishments. Strong, double-stick tape works in small areas for paper and some low-profile embellishments. Low-tack, repositionable tape temporarily adheres templates or patterns.

Choose good-quality brushes with dense, tight bristles for applying glue. A foam brush can be used, but it soaks up glue, making it difficult to determine how much is in the brush.

RULERS

Metal-edge rulers in 12″ and 18″ (30.5 cm and 45.7 cm) lengths are best for measuring and cutting; hold the ruler firmly and cut directly against the edge with a craft or utility knife. Heavier materials may require several passes to cut all the way through. Cork-backed metal rulers prevent slipping, but knife blades may get caught in the gap created by the cork, resulting in imperfect cuts. It's better to back a metal ruler with 300-grit sandpaper; glue the sandpaper with PVA and press until dry.

TOOL UPGRADES

These tools are more expensive, but often worth the cost.

- Electric or battery-powered hand drill: A quick, efficient way to make holes in thick book board, wood, and metal.
- Japanese screw punch: Creates holes of various sizes anywhere in paper, cardstock, or book board. The smooth ratchet drill requires little effort.
- Teflon bone folder: Won't leave marks while smoothing paper or book cloth.

Basic Tool Kit

A bookbinder's basic tool kit should include the following items. Always keep these tools close by when making a book—they're essential and will be used in some combination in every project.

- craft knife
- utility knife
- bone folder
- awl
- scissors
- metal ruler
- cutting mat
- glue brush
- needles
- pencil
- eraser

▶ **Top left: A**, PVA; **B**, thick craft glue; **C**, glue stick; **D**, low-tack repositionable tape; **E**, bone folder; **F**, double-stick tape; **G**, foam brush; **H**, standard glue brush. **Top right: I**, 18″ metal ruler; **J**, 12″ metal ruler backed with sandpaper. **Bottom: K**, electric hand drill; **L**, Japanese screw punch with tips; **M**, Teflon bone folder.

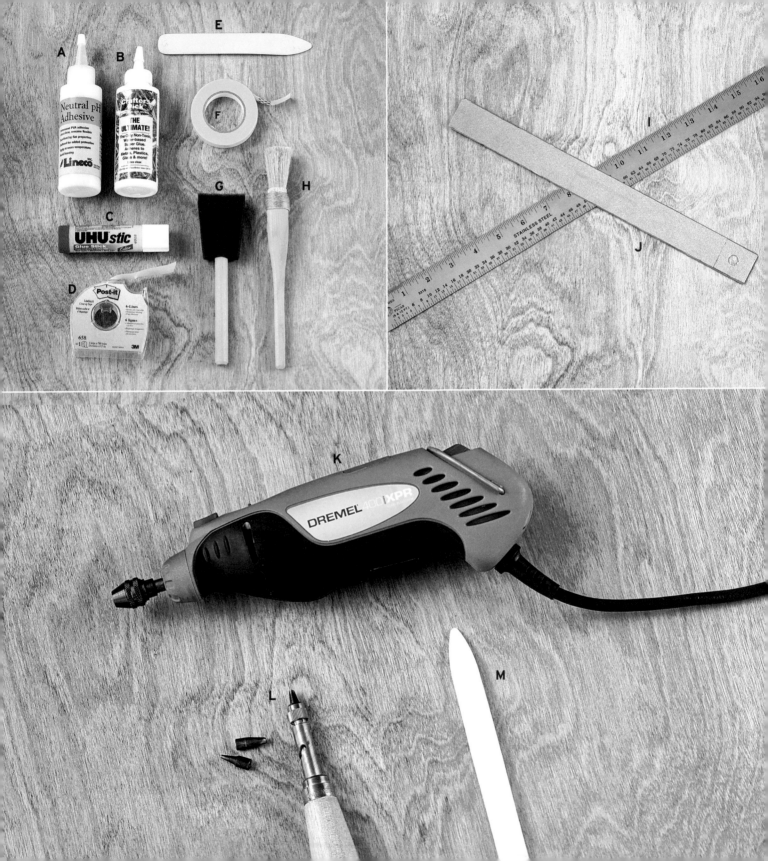

Guidelines

These tips will be useful with almost every project, and with practice, the techniques will eventually become second nature.

PAPER GRAIN

All machine-made paper has a grain, which refers to the direction in which the paper fibers line up during manufacturing. When buying reams of machine-made paper, the grain direction will be printed on the package as grain short, or GS (grain runs along the paper's short side), or grain long, or GL (grain runs along the paper's long side).

Grain is important when folding paper—fold with the grain for a smooth crease. Folding against the grain breaks the paper fibers and results in a bumpy crease, which may eventually tear. When folding paper for signatures or when making an accordion fold, always fold with the grain. Grain direction is given for projects in this book when appropriate.

To determine grain direction, hold two sides of a piece of paper in both hands and bend it slightly. Hold the other two sides and bend it again. The direction offering the least resistance is the grain direction.

Grain direction may be difficult or impossible to establish when working with recycled materials. Make judgments based on the book's structure and purpose, testing the materials whenever possible.

▶ Cabinet-card Sketchbook with stab binding, page 45

SCORING

Scoring prepares paper to be folded—especially heavy-weight paper or cardstock—and creates cleaner folds. Mark the score line at the paper edges, and then align a metal-edge ruler with the marks as a guide. Impress or deboss a line into the paper with the pointed end of a bone folder, an empty ballpoint pen, or a scoring tool (a wood or plastic handle with a small metal ball on the end) held against the ruler. Don't press too hard or the paper may tear. Fold along the score line.

SEWING

Prepare the signatures before binding the book together. The pages, or folios, are folded and nested together to form each signature. A signature-punching template is then used to mark where the holes are to be punched in the folded paper to allow for easy sewing. Slip the template into the center of a signature, open the signature at 45 degrees, hold the awl parallel to the table, and punch straight through, making sure you come out exactly on the crease **(A)**. For multiple signatures, remove the template and repeat. Check every few signatures to make sure the holes are aligned.

If signatures are being sewn directly to the spine, the holes on the spine-punching template must match the holes on the signature-punching template.

Signatures can be sewn in various ways using a single thread strand. Each stitch offers a distinct look and determines how the book will open, whether completely flat, or with pages and covers that bend back. Different bindings will be covered in each project. When designing a book, consider the book's style and function when determining which type of binding and stitches to use.

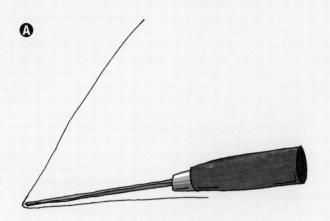

Punch signature holes with an awl.

GLUING

Strive to spread a thin, even layer of glue, and work from the center of the page to the outside edges. When applying glue to paper, the paper may start to curl as it reacts to the moisture. Keep working the glue into the paper—without adding more—and it will eventually relax. If book board warps after being glued, press it under weights.

MODELS

The key to creating eye-catching and functional books is to first make a model, especially when working with unfamiliar materials or bindings. This ensures that everything, from the page height to the closure, will result as envisioned. Whenever possible, work with the actual materials, such as record albums (use the backs) or felted sweaters (use scraps). If that's unfeasible, replicate the materials as closely as possible. Keep notes on what does and doesn't work.

Thoughts on Archival Materials

Making quality books that last for years is the goal of almost every bookbinder and book artist. Seeing pages yellow or glue start to flake is disheartening, so every effort is made to incorporate archival materials that are pH neutral and noncorrosive, and paper that is free of lignin, which makes it brittle.

But when it comes to some recycled and repurposed items, all bets are off. While the projects in this book are sturdy and use some archival materials, they're also meant to be fun, to be eco-friendly, and to push creative boundaries. However, some items, such as cabinet cards, have been around for more than a hundred years, so they may very well last another hundred.

The following books present a variety of materials, styles, and bindings, and use items easily found at home and in flea markets, thrift shops, hardware and office-supply stores, and dumpsters, and even stuff that's free. But this is only a fraction of what the world holds. Remember to keep eyes and minds open to the possibilities of what can be a book.

CHAPTER 2

There's No Place Like Home— To Make a Book

Within every junk drawer, behind every cabinet door, lurking in every closet, are the ingredients for making amazing one-of-a-kind books. Spotting those materials, however, requires seeing commonplace items with new eyes.

An empty box of pancake mix is the perfect cover for a recipe journal, which is bound with a long stitch. Broken kitchen gadgets, once disassembled, are handy closures or embellishments. Paper grocery bags are durable text pages (but will become brittle over time). And that's just what the kitchen has to offer.

In the office, an old decorative file folder gets a new life as a pocket notebook. Junk mail envelopes are turned inside out, and the patterned paper is used for book pages. Last year's wall calendar becomes a distinctive photo album.

Every clothes closet has its worn, outdated, or outgrown garments, but they don't have to be tossed or given away. Sort through to see what can be salvaged, like the leather briefcase, circa 1997, that can be turned into an address book. A pair of once-trendy jeans is still good for something—those pockets can grace the cover of a journal.

Don't forget the bathroom—it can yield gems such as rugs, shower curtains, towels, and hot-water bottles, all destined for greatness by being made into books.

Get in the habit of giving objects a once-over to determine whether anything can be rescued before relegating it to the trash pile. A crooked frame may just need some glue or a nail, and then it's off to be made into a book. Even if inspiration doesn't strike immediately, keep potentially useful bits in a box and see what transpires later. Write ideas or sketches on sticky notes and attach them to the item if the project can't be tackled right away.

Of course, not everything is fair game—a child's favorite stuffed animal might make a fantastic mini book, but it's probably not worth the tantrum. Check with family members before deconstructing their possessions.

In this chapter, a hot-water bottle finds new life as a take-along journal, which is bound with an eye-catching cross-stitch, and very little of the bottle is wasted. The bold, colorful graphics of snack-chip bags become the cover of a two-part notebook that takes only minutes to bind with a quick pamphlet stitch. And a bathroom rug is laundered and made over into a button-bound journal with pages that expand in surprising ways.

Hot-Water Bottle Journal

BINDING STYLE: **CROSS-STITCH** | APPROXIMATE FINISHED SIZE: 4″ x 6″ (10.2 x 15.2 cm)

Hot-water bottles are comforting companions on blustery days, but when they spring a small leak or outlive their usefulness, honor them by making them into take-along journals. The rubber makes a strong, flexible, and waterproof cover, and the book is roomy inside, perfect for adding pictures, pockets, and ephemera. The pages open flat for easy writing, and the closure is made from the bottle's funnel top. Use contrasting thread to show off the attractive binding stitches.

Materials

- hot-water bottle, approximately 7″ x 12″ (17.8 x 30.5 cm)
- sixteen 6½″ x 5¾″ (16.5 x 14.6 cm) sheets text-weight paper for the text block, grain short (Fold the pages in half and nest into four signatures of four folios each; round the corners.)
- two 30″ (76.2 cm) pieces waxed linen thread in contrasting color to hot-water bottle
- 2 rivets and rivet-setting tools
- snap and snap-setting tools
- pinking shears (optional)
- repositionable low-tack tape
- signature-punching template (page 124)
- cover-punching template (page 124)

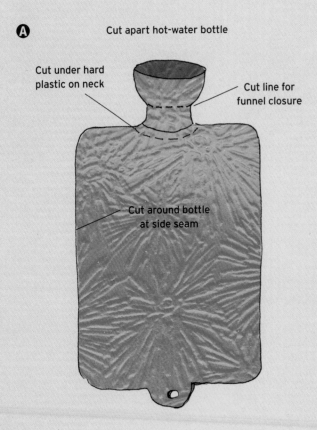

Ⓐ Cut apart hot-water bottle

Cut under hard plastic on neck

Cut line for funnel closure

Cut around bottle at side seam

Prepare the Cover

1. Cut around the perimeter of the hot-water bottle along the seam. Cut under the bottle's hard plastic neck, but leave the funnel intact, and set it aside **(A)**. With a utility knife and metal ruler, cut an 8″ x 6″ (20.3 x 15.2 cm) rectangle from the bottle, and then round the corners (see "Tips" at right).

TIPS
- Round off the cover corners with scissors, tracing around a coin as a guide.
- Smooth the rough rubber edges with a disposable razor. Use even strokes to shave the edges after cutting them into the desired rounded shape.

Sew the Book

1. Copy or trace the signature-punching template on page 124, and then punch all four signatures.

2. Copy or trace the cover-punching template on page 124, center it inside the cover, and secure with repositionable tape. Punch the holes using an awl or a Japanese screw punch fitted with the 1-mm tip.

3. The signatures are bound to the cover so all the sewing goes through the signatures and the cover. Thread a needle with 30″ (76.2 cm) of waxed linen thread. Enter the first signature through hole #1 from the inside, and then go through the corresponding hole on the cover, leaving a 3″ (7.6 cm) tail. Enter hole #2 on the cover, pick up the second signature and enter it through hole #2 from the outside; keep stitches loose. Exit the second signature through hole #3 from the inside, and then through the cover. Enter hole #4 from the outside, and then into the first signature **(B)**. Tighten the stitching by pulling both ends of the thread parallel to the spine. Tie a square knot at hole #4 using the thread and thread tail. Do not trim the thread ends.

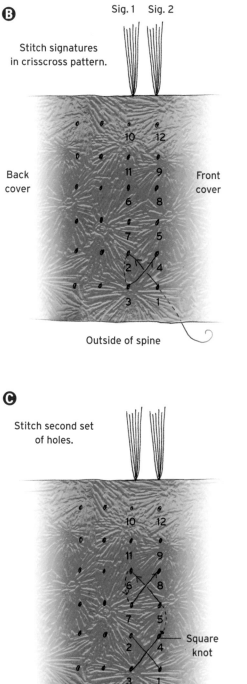

B

Sig. 1   Sig. 2

Stitch signatures in crisscross pattern.

Back cover

Front cover

Outside of spine

4. Keep the thread taut for the remainder of the sewing. Enter the first signature in hole #5 from the inside and enter the second signature in hole #6 from the outside. Exit the second signature through hole #7 and enter the first signature in hole #8 from the outside **(C)**. Exit the first signature through hole #9 from the inside, and then enter the second signature in hole #10 from the outside. Exit the second signature through hole #11 from the inside, and enter the first signature in hole #12 from the outside **(D)**.

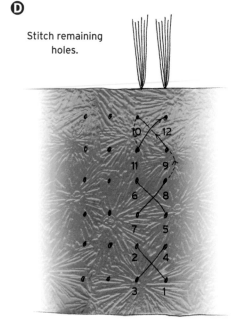

C

Stitch second set of holes.

Square knot

D

Stitch remaining holes.

5. Knot the thread by slipping the needle under the last stitch on the inside of the first signature, and pull the thread toward the head of the book until it is taut **(E)**. Slide the needle under the stitch again from the same direction and pull the thread until a small loop forms. Go through the loop with the needle and pull toward the head of the book until a knot forms at hole #12 **(F)**. Repeat, forming one more loop, and knot. Trim this thread and tail end to ¼˝ (6 mm). Repeat this sequence to sew and tie the third and fourth signatures.

E

Inside signature #1

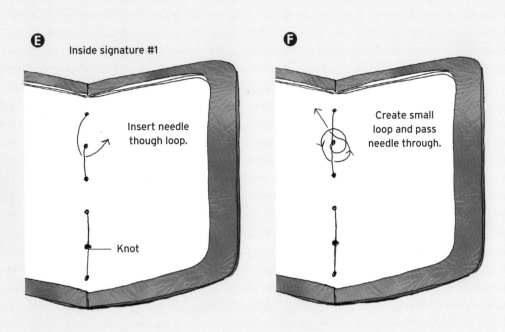

Insert needle though loop.

Knot

F

Create small loop and pass needle through.

Attach the Closure

1. Cut the funnel piece along one side seam, and then cut along the bottom (above the hard plastic neck), preserving any writing. Open the piece out flat and trim to 6˝ x 1¼˝ (15.2 x 3.1 cm). Trim the lower edge with pinking shears if desired. Since the funnel piece is curved, place the center along the straight fore edge and allow the ends to curve down across the cover front and back. Attach the back with two rivets following the manufacturer's instructions **(G)**. Attach the snap fastener to the opposite end and the front cover, following the manufacturer's instructions.

G

Attach closure strip to back cover.

TRY THIS
Bath mats are also made of rubber and make great book covers; I would suggest using a new one.

Bath Rug Idea Journal

BINDING STYLE: HIDDEN LONG-STITCH BUTTON BINDING | APPROXIMATE FINISHED SIZE: 5 ½″ x 6″ (14 x 15.2 cm)

Fresh from the washer and dryer, bathroom rugs rescued from the floor can be turned into idea journals. The thick, textural material is ideal for protecting the contents inside. Almost every element of this book can be found around the house, from the file folders and grocery bags that serve as pages, to an old necklace and leash clip that make up the closure. Expandable pages are perfect for documenting big ideas—the extra room is suitable for creating mood boards, making art-journal pages, or adding photos. An easy button binding hides all the stitching so only the decorative buttons show. One more surprise: a pocket made from a shower curtain.

Materials

- 12″ x 6″ (30.5 x 15.2 cm) rectangle from double-sided bathroom rug made of cotton or cotton/rayon with loop pile on one side and straight pile on the other
- 40″ (1 m) of 1″ (2.5 cm) -wide seam binding, linen tape, or twill tape
- three 10″ x 5″ (25.4 x 12.7 cm) rectangles from decorative file folders, folded in half crosswise
- three 10″ x 5″ (25.4 x 12.7 cm) rectangles from grocery bags, folded in half crosswise
- two 10″ (25.4 cm) cardstock squares for expandable pages
- 14¾″ x 15″ (37.4 x 38.1 cm) cardstock rectangle for expandable page
- 3½″ x 8¼″ (8.9 x 21 cm) rectangle of shower curtain for pocket
- 9 sew-through ½″ (1.3 cm) buttons
- approximately forty 5-mm beads with large hole
- approximately 3″ (7.6 cm) of large link chain
- large spring clasp (as found on dog leash or key fob)
- monofilament (a strong, thin, transparent polymer thread used for jewelry)
- three 24″ (61 cm) lengths of waxed linen thread
- sewing thread to match seam binding
- sewing needle
- bookbinding needle
- straight pins
- strong double-stick tape
- low-tack painter's tape
- signature-punching template (page 125)

Prepare the Cover

1. Remove any loose rug fibers from the 12″ x 6″ (30.5 x 15.2 cm) rug piece. Beginning on the lower long edge of the back cover, insert the rug into the fold of the seam binding, and then pin the binding to each side of the rug, placing pins parallel to the edge. At the corners, fold and tuck in the excess so the seam binding lies flat; pin (A). Stop pinning just before the seam-binding end. Use a needle or an awl to pull out any rug pile tucked underneath the seam binding.

2. Thread the sewing needle, and knot the end. Starting at the beginning of the seam binding, take a small stitch into the rug just above the seam binding, catching the canvas in the middle, not just the pile. Then take a stitch into the seam binding's inner edge. Take another small stitch into the rug and seam binding about ½″ (1.3 cm) away; pull the thread taut (B). Continue in this manner to sew the seam binding to the rug, stopping 1½″ (3.8 cm) from the seam-binding end. Repeat to sew the binding to the other side of the rug. Overlap the seam binding ends about 1½″ (3.8 cm), fold the raw end under ½″ (1.3 cm), and stitch in place (C).

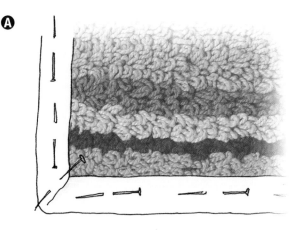

Pin binding to rug rectangle.

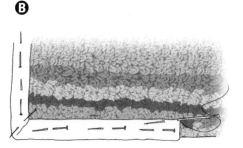

Stitch binding to rug.

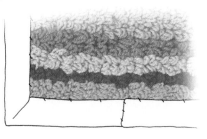

Fold under raw end and overlap to finish.

3. Thread the sewing needle with monofilament, and knot the ends together. Take a small stitch into the inner edge of the seam binding on the front cover, hiding the knot underneath the binding. Thread a bead onto the needle and tack it in place. Take another small stitch into the binding and come out ½″ (1.3 cm) away, thread a bead onto the needle, and tack it in place. Repeat to add beads all the way around the cover.

TRY THIS

- Add drama with rhinestone buttons on a black rug.
- Use wide decorative ribbon instead of the seam binding.
- Go natural with wood, shell, and horn buttons and nubby linen twill tape.
- Experiment with other types of long-stitch bindings.

Prepare the Signatures

1. Place a 10″ (25.4 cm) cardstock square on your work surface. Score and fold the square in half, unfold, and then score and fold it in half again, bringing the other edges together. Turn the square over, and score and fold it once diagonally. Hold the cardstock so that the diagonal fold forms a peak, and the other folds form valleys. Bring the diagonal-fold corners toward each other, which causes the remaining two corners to pull in toward the center, creating a smaller folded square. Open up the page and mark the signature-punching holes **(D)**.

2. Score and fold the other 10″ (25.4 cm) cardstock square in half, unfold, and then fold in half again, bringing the other edges together. Open the page and with the page positioned so the folds resemble a cross, draw a parallel line ⅛″ (3 mm) below the left half of the horizontal fold. Remove the ⅛″ (3 mm) -wide section with a craft knife. Mark the signature-punching holes **(E)**. To close the page, A folds over to B, which folds up to C, and closes with D.

3. Prepare the 14 ¾″ x 15″ (37.4 x 38.1 cm) cardstock rectangle. Referring to the signature-punching template on page 125, remove the corner sections from the rectangle, leaving a cross shape. Score and fold the

lines created by connecting the inner corners. Score and fold another line on the C and D sections, ⅛″ (3 mm) outward from the previous fold. On section A, cut two lines that are perpendicular to the fold. Mark the signature-punching holes on the B-section fold. To close this page, fold in A and B toward the center square, fold in C, and then D.

4. Assemble each signature from the outside as follows: file-folder page, grocery-bag page, and expandable page. Open up the expandable pages, and punch the signatures at the marked locations.

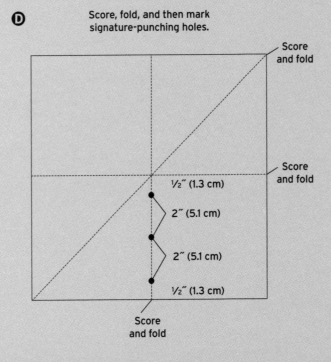

D Score, fold, and then mark signature-punching holes.

Score and fold

Score and fold

½″ (1.3 cm)

2″ (5.1 cm)

2″ (5.1 cm)

½″ (1.3 cm)

Score and fold

TIPS

- For straighter lines when cutting, use low-tack painter's tape to outline the cover dimensions on the rug.

- Recycle old jewelry pieces into embellishments and closures. Beads, charms, chains, pins, and earrings look great adorning books.

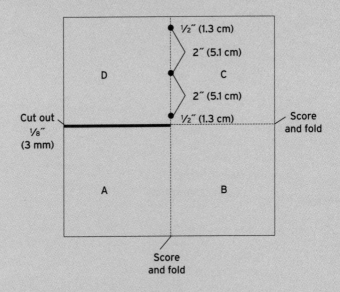

E Score, fold, and mark signature-punching holes.

½″ (1.3 cm)

2″ (5.1 cm)

D   C

2″ (5.1 cm)

Cut out ⅛″ (3 mm)

½″ (1.3 cm)   Score and fold

A   B

Score and fold

Sew the Book

1. The signatures are sewn directly to the cover. Open the cover and mark the center fold with straight pins at the head and tail edges. The rug is difficult to mark; place a piece of low-tack painter's tape across the cover aligned with the pins; remove the pins. The tape's right edge is the sewing guide for the bookbinding. Thread the bookbinding needle with 24˝ (61 cm) of waxed linen thread. Center one signature on the cover aligned with the tape edge (G), and then open the expandable page. Enter the top hole from the inside and exit through the cover. Make sure the needle goes only through the canvas, not through the rug pile, which will make sewing difficult. Insert the needle through both holes of a button (H). Remove the needle, and then tie a square knot underneath the button using only as much thread as necessary, leaving the rest for the binding. Trim the thread end to ¼˝ (6 mm). Rethread the needle onto the other thread end, and pull the button flush with the cover.

2. Enter the middle hole, staying aligned with the tape, and exit through the cover. Insert the needle through both holes of another button, and then go back into the cover very close to where the thread

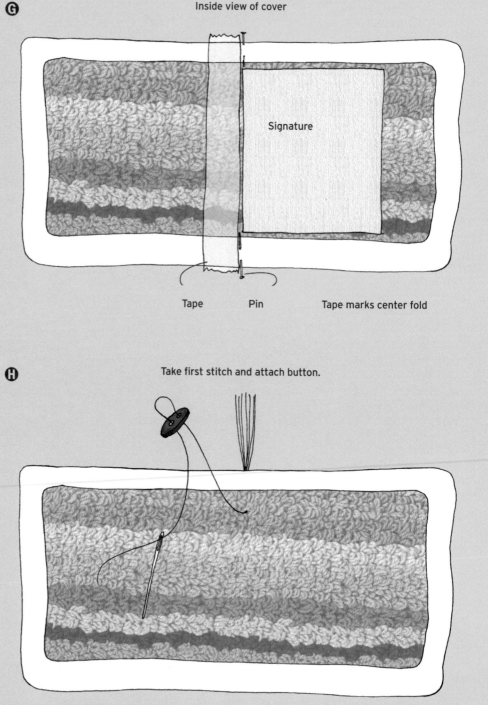

G   Inside view of cover

Signature

Tape   Pin   Tape marks center fold

H   Take first stitch and attach button.

exited, but not in the same spot **(I)**. Enter the signature, pull the button flush to the cover, and then pull the thread parallel to the spine to tighten.

3. Enter the bottom hole of the signature, go through the cover, thread on a button, go back into the cover close to where the thread exited, enter the signature, pull the button flush, and then pull the thread parallel to the spine to tighten. Slip the needle under the lower stitch until a loop forms. Insert the needle through the loop and pull down, forming a knot **(J)**. Repeat to make another knot; trim the end to ¼˝ (6 mm).

4. Inside the cover, measure ⅜˝ (1 cm) to the left of the center signature, and mark with pins at the head and tail edges. Align low-tack painter's tape just left of the pins; remove the pins. Line up another signature with the tape's right edge and the previously sewn signature; sew the signature to the cover.

5. Measure ⅜˝ (1 cm) to the right of the center signature, and mark with pins at the head and tail edges. Align low-tack painter's tape just to the right of the pins. Line up the remaining signature along the tape's left edge and with the previous two signatures; repeat the sewing.

I Take second stitch and add button.

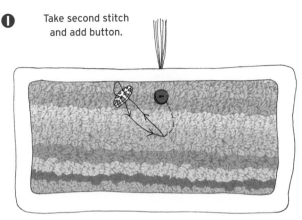

J

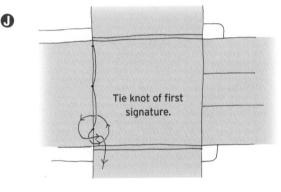

Tie knot of first signature.

Make the Closure

1. Find the center point of the front and back cover fore edge, and mark with pins. Sew the spring/clasp closure to the back cover at the pin mark. Determine the chain length needed, and then use the monofilament to sew the chain to the front cover fore edge at the pin, wrapping around the last link several times to secure.

Shower-Curtain Pocket

1. The pocket shown uses the shower-curtain edge with the grommet for one short edge of the rectangle. Fold up the rectangle opposite the short edge ¼˝ (6 mm) to the wrong side, finger press, and then sew in place. (If the grommet edge wasn't used, fold up both short ends and sew in place.) Fold the piece in half with the wrong sides facing and align the short ends; sew the sides together by hand or machine. Attach the pocket to a page using strong double-stick tape.

Potato-Chip Bag Double-Sided Notebook

BINDING STYLE: **DOUBLE PAMPHLET STITCH**
APPROXIMATE FINISHED SIZE: **5″ x 7″ (12.7 x 17.8 cm)**

Chip bags have bold, colorful designs that make striking book covers. While the bags are strong, they're also extremely lightweight. Reinforce the bags with Tyvek to gain heft while staying flexible. The two-part construction of this book and the handy pencil closure make it perfect for jotting quick notes. Be sure to use only foil-lined chip bags.

Materials

- two 11″ x 2¾″ (27.9 x 7 cm) chip bag rectangles for cover
- 11″ x 2½″ (28 x 6.5 cm) chip bag rectangle for cover
- 9¾″ x 6¾″ (25.7 x 17 cm) chip bag rectangle for cover lining
- two 1¼″ x 2¼″ (3.1 x 5.6 cm) chip bag rectangles for closure
- 10″ x 7″ (25.4 x 17.8 cm) Tyvek rectangle for cover
- two ½″ x 2¼″ (1.3 x 5.7 cm) Tyvek rectangles for closure
- 28″ (71.1 cm) of waxed linen thread
- bookbinding needle
- nine 8″ x 6¾″ (20.3 x 17.1 cm) sheets loose-leaf paper, folded in half widthwise (Reserve one folio for signature-punching template; nest remaining into one signature.)
- eight 8″ x 6¾″ (20.3 x 17.1 cm) sheets graph paper, folded in half and nested into one signature
- glue stick
- sewing machine or needle and thread

TIP

To clean the chip bags, cut off the upper and lower seams, and then cut open the back seam. Wash with warm soapy water to remove oil and crumbs. Dry with a cloth or paper towel to avoid water spots.

TRY THIS

- Use candy wrappers instead of chip bags.
- Vary the size and arrangement of the graphics.
- If using a sewing machine with decorative-stitch features, try different stitches around the cover perimeter using a contrasting color thread.

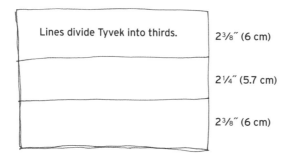

A Lines divide Tyvek into thirds.

2⅜″ (6 cm)

2¼″ (5.7 cm)

2⅜″ (6 cm)

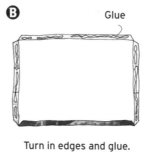

B Glue

Turn in edges and glue.

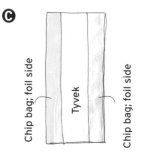

C Chip bag; foil side | Tyvek | Chip bag; foil side

Glue these pieces together.

Make the Cover

1. Mark the large Tyvek cover rectangle 2⅜″ (6 cm) from both long edges and draw two parallel pencil lines across the page at the marks, dividing the rectangle into three sections (the middle section should measure 2¼″ [5.7 cm]) **(A)**. Apply glue stick to the upper third of the Tyvek and attach one 11″ x 2¾″ (27.9 x 7 cm) chip-bag rectangle, allowing ½″ (1.3 cm) to overhang on three sides. Do the same on the lower third with the other same size chip-bag rectangle. Apply glue to the foil side of the 11 x 2½″ (27.9 x 6.4 cm) chip-bag rectangle and place it in the middle, overlapping the other two sections by ⅛″ (3 mm) and extending ½″ (1.3 cm) on either side.

2. Turn the piece over and trim the corners on the diagonal, leaving ⅛″ (3 mm) past the Tyvek. Apply glue to the chip-bag overhanging edges, fold in, and crease with a bone folder **(B)**.

3. For the closure, center and glue each ½″ x 2¼″ (1.3 x 5.7 cm) Tyvek rectangle to the foil side of each 1¼″ x 2¼″ (3.1 x 5.6 cm) chip-bag rectangle **(C)**. Apply glue to the foil side of the overhanging chip bag, and fold toward the center; the turned-in edges will overlap a bit. Stitch down the lengthwise center of each closure by hand or machine. Fold each strip in half with the overlapping edges on the inside, and align the short ends. With the inside cover face up, pencil-mark the midpoints of the left and right fore edges. Position one closure on the right side just above the midpoint and the other on the left side just below the midpoint; secure with a little glue **(D)**. Make sure the closures can accommodate a pen or pencil and they don't overlap when the book is closed. Glue the foil side of the 9¾″ x 6¾″ (24.9 x 17.2 cm) chip-bag rectangle to the inside cover. Sew around the cover perimeter by hand or machine, capturing the closures in the stitching.

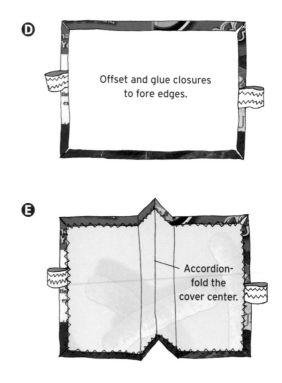

D Offset and glue closures to fore edges.

E Accordion-fold the cover center.

4. Fold the cover in half with right sides facing; crease the fold. Measure ½″ (1.3 cm) on either side of the fold, and then fold the cover the opposite way along each fold so wrong sides are facing, creating an accordion fold **(E)**.

Sew the Book

1. Make the signature-punching template with the reserved 8″ x 6 ¾″ (20.3 x 17.1 cm) sheet of paper. Fold the paper in half widthwise, mark the fold ¾″ (2 cm) from the upper and lower edges, and 3 ⅜″ (8.6 cm) from the upper edge. Fold the cover along the center fold so right sides are facing and the other folds are aligned—these folds are where the signatures will be sewn. Open the template, center it along one fold, and punch the holes through all layers (**F**). Slip the template into the center of each signature and punch holes. Refold the book with wrong sides facing, and place a signature in each fold on the inside.

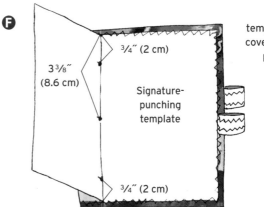

F

¾″ (2 cm)

3 ⅜″
(8.6 cm)

Signature-punching template

¾″ (2 cm)

Align template with cover fold and punch.

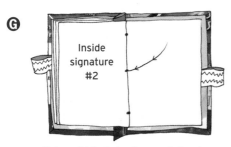

G

Inside signature #2

Enter middle hole of second signature

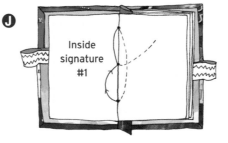

J

Inside signature #1

Enter middle of first signature

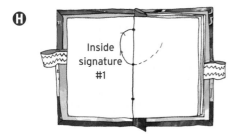

H

Inside signature #1

Enter top of first signature

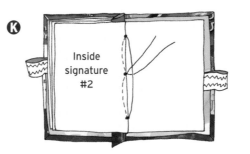

K

Inside signature #2

Arrange a thread on each side of long stitch

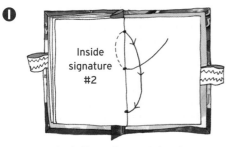

I

Inside signature #2

Enter bottom of second signature

2. The two signatures will be sewn to the cover at the same time. This structure is also known as two-sewn-as-one. Thread the bookbinding needle and enter the middle hole in the second signature from the inside (**G**), pass through the cover, and enter the middle hole of the first signature, leaving a 4″ (10.2 cm) tail (**H**). Enter the top hole of the first signature, pass through the cover, and then enter the top hole of the second signature. Enter the bottom hole of the second signature (**I**), go through the cover, and into the first signature. Enter the middle hole of the first signature (**J**), go through the cover, and then into the middle hole of the second signature, coming out on one side of the long stitch, opposite the thread tail (**K**). Take up any slack in the threads by pulling them parallel to the spine. Tie the thread ends in a square knot and trim to ¼″ (6 mm).

CHAPTER 3

Hunting Buried Treasure: Flea Markets and Thrift Stores

Flea markets, thrift stores, and garage sales are gold mines for book artists. Record-album covers, handbags, cigar-box lids, chocolate molds, and tin ceiling tiles are just a few of the unusual items that can be turned into books, portfolios, and photo albums. Since many of these pieces have experienced wear and tear, it is important to assess their quality and adaptability before purchasing.

Chip-board items, such as cabinet-card photographs and record-album covers, must be sturdy, not bent, and free of tears or holes that could compromise the book structure. Leather clothing and accessories shouldn't be degraded; gently stretch the material and hold it up to a light to determine its strength and durability. A little rust on metal is fine (it can be sealed with a spray sealer), but avoid anything with severe corrosion. Fabrics and trims, such as lace and crocheted pieces, should also be in good shape. Stains can be covered with embellishments, but thin, flimsy fibers may not stand up to constant handling. Check that wood pieces aren't rotted or warped. Store vintage items in a zip-top plastic bag for a couple of days to make sure they are bug-free. Remember though, that moderate signs of age and wear and tear are a good thing and add to the book's style and charm.

When buying something for a specific purpose, make sure it is up to the job. If a leather belt is to become a closure, is it flexible enough to bend around a book? Are antique ledger sheets too brittle to work as text pages?

Oddly shaped dimensional items may not be suitable for book covers, but they do make distinctive embellishments. Look for vintage rulers, yardsticks, jewelry, tatting, medals, buttons, and hardware. Think about how they can be attached, either by glue or wire, or by drilling holes and securing with brads, eyelets, screws, or rivets.

When it comes to purchasing items, thrift stores usually have set prices. At flea markets and garage sales, however, negotiating a fair price is an expected part of the transaction. Although the process makes some people uncomfortable, it shouldn't be stressful, and after a couple of purchases it will feel completely natural. Above all, maintain a poker face. Being overly enthusiastic can drive up the cost. Determine how much an item is worth, and then ask the price. If the cost is in the ballpark, the negotiation begins. Offering the seller 20 to 30 percent less will result in an agreement, a flat-out refusal, or a compromise. A refusal doesn't always mean no; putting an item down and walking away can sometimes prompt a seller to come back with a better price. Merchandise under five dollars is usually not worth haggling over, but do bargain for multiple low-priced items. Don't insult sellers by offering half of the asking price.

When seeking specific or hard-to-find pieces, such as large tintypes, get to know vendors who specialize in those items. Many are happy to hunt for them.

Online auction sites may have made it easier to search for vintage goods, but nothing beats the thrill of the chase and the element of surprise that flea markets and thrift stores offer. Keeping an open mind to how treasures can be reworked will no doubt result in amazing books.

The three projects in this chapter transform easy-to-find items into distinctive structures. With the help of a washer and dryer, a wool sweater is felted and becomes a long-stitch journal with a cover for showcasing elaborate embroidery. Cabinet-card photographs, connected with a simple cross-stitch, open to reveal two notebooks bound with an attractive and simple stab binding. Retro record albums turn into a handsome portfolio dressed up with an antique doorknob.

Vintage Album-Cover Portfolio

BINDING STYLE: **JUMP-RING HINGE**
APPROXIMATE FINISHED SIZE: 8″ x 11″ (20.3 x 27.9 cm)

Vintage record albums may have gone the way of the rotary-dial telephone, but their artistry endures. Well-known artists such as Andy Warhol, Salvador Dali, Wassily Kandinsky, and Robert Rauschenberg contributed their work to a number of stunning covers, as did other artists and photographers.

Today, vintage albums are inexpensive—usually under five dollars—and can easily be found at thrift stores and flea markets. This five-piece portfolio shows off elements from several covers and incorporates other vintage items such as candy and ice-cream packages, labels, and postcards. The frames and backgrounds are made from printed and rubber-stamped cardstock, and the book is hinged with jump rings, which can be recycled from a necklace.

TIPS
- Some vintage record albums are made from chipboard with a high acid content. If concerned, spray the chipboard with a de-acidifier, and use archival cardstock.
- Check the albums for liner notes and record sleeves. They often feature retro photographs and graphics, which can be incorporated into the portfolio.

Materials
- 8″ x 11″ (20.3 x 27.9 cm) album-cover rectangle
- two 5½″ x 10½″ (14 x 26.7 cm) album-cover rectangles
- two 7½″ x 5⅜″ (19.1 x 13.7 cm) album-cover rectangles, trim using curved-panel pattern (page 126)
- 8″ x 11″ (20.3 x 27.9 cm) cardstock rectangle for liner
- two 5½″ x 10″ (14 x 25.4 cm) cardstock rectangles for liner
- two 7½″ x 5⅜″ (19.1 x 13.7 cm) cardstock rectangles for liner, trim using curved-panel pattern (page 126)
- 7″ x 10″ (17.8 x 25.4 cm) cardstock rectangle for frame
- 6″ x 9″ (15.2 x 22.9 cm) cardstock rectangle for frame
- four 1″ x 1″ x 1⅜″ (2.5 x 2.5 x 3.5 cm) cardstock triangles
- four 4″ x 6″ (10.2 x 15.2 cm) cardstock rectangles for side panel flip-ups (if using vintage ephemera, it should be no larger than 4″ x 7″ [10.2 x 17.8 cm])
- four 4″ x 5½″ (10.2 x 14 cm) cardstock rectangles for flip-up liners
- two 3½″ x 5½″ (8.9 x 14 cm) postcards
- 1″ x 3½″ (2.5 x 8.9 cm) cardstock strip for postcard hinge
- thirty-six ⅛″ (3 mm) eyelets, eyelet-setting tools
- ⅛″ (3 mm) hole punch or Japanese screw punch fitted with a 2.5-mm tip
- approximately twenty-eight 12-mm jump rings for hinges
- small vintage drawer knob for closure
- 30″ (76.2 cm) of ⅝″ (1.6 cm) -wide ribbon for closure
- four 10″ (25.4 cm) pieces of ⅝″ (1.6 cm) -wide twill tape or ribbon for flip-ups
- PVA and glue stick
- ½″ (1.3 cm) -wide strong double-stick tape
- center-panel punching template (page 126)
- side-panel punching template (page 127)

Make the Portfolio

1. Measure 1″ (2.5 cm) from all four sides of the 7″ x 10″ (17.8 x 25.4 cm) and the 6″ x 9″ (15.2 x 22.9 cm) cardstock rectangles, and draw a light pencil line. Cut out the inner rectangles, leaving 1″ (2.5 cm) -wide frames.

2. Measure ½″ and 1″ (1.3 cm and 2.5 cm) from all sides of the 8″ x 11″ (20.3 x 27.9 cm) cardstock rectangle. Draw a rectangle with pencil to connect the ½″ (1.3 cm) marks, and draw a rectangle to connect the 1″ (2.5 cm) marks. Apply double-stick tape around the perimeter of the smaller frame on the wrong side. Using the smaller rectangle lines as a guide, adhere the frame to the cardstock.

3. Apply double-stick tape to the perimeter of the larger frame on the wrong side. Using the outer lines as a guide, adhere the larger frame over the smaller frame; ½″ of the underneath frame should show. Apply glue stick to the cardstock triangles and attach one to each corner of the frame. Apply PVA to the wrong side of the 8″ x 11″ (20.3 x 27.9 cm) album-cover rectangle and adhere it to the back of the cardstock with the frames. Press the assemblage under heavy weight if it warps.

4. Score one 4″ x 6″ (10.2 x 15.2 cm) cardstock rectangle ½″ (1.3 cm) from one short edge; fold along the score. Repeat for the remaining three same-size rectangles.

5. Create the portfolio flip-up sections. On one 5½″ x 10½″ (14 x 26.7 cm) cardstock rectangle use a craft knife to cut two 4″ (10.2 cm) slits. Center each slit ½″ (1.3 cm) from and parallel to the short edges (A). Slip the ½″ (1.3 cm) folded tabs of two 4″ x 6″ (10.2 x 15.2 cm) rectangles through the slits and adhere the tabs to the wrong side with a glue stick or double-stick tape. Repeat with the remaining 4″ x 6″ (10.2 x 15.2 cm) and 5½″ x 10½″ (14 x 26.7 cm) rectangles.

6. Fold the flip-up sections toward each other, and measure ¼″ (6 mm) on either side of where they overlap, and then cut ⅝″ (1.6 cm) slits to accommodate the ribbon. Insert a 10″ (25.4 cm) ribbon into each slit ½″ (1.3 cm) and glue in place on the underside. Apply PVA to the four 4″ x 5½″ (10.2 x 14 cm) cardstock rectangles and glue to the undersides of the flip-up sections, covering the ribbon ends

7. Apply PVA to the wrong side of one 5½″ x 10½″ (14 x 26.7 cm) album-cover rectangle and adhere it to back of the same-size cardstock rectangle. Repeat with the other 5½″ x 10½″ (14 x 26.7 cm) album-cover rectangle.

8. Score the lengthwise center of the 1″ x 3½″ (2.5 x 8.9 cm) cardstock strip to make a postcard hinge; fold along the score. Adhere half of the hinge to the left short edge of the postcard on the underside. Cut a 3½″ (8.9 cm) slit parallel to and 1″ (2.5 cm) from the left side of one curved cardstock panel, which will become the upper portion of the portfolio. Slip the other half of the hinge into the slit and adhere it to the back of the curved panel. Apply PVA to the wrong side of the curved album-cover panel and adhere it to the corresponding piece of cardstock with the hinged postcard. The other postcard is simply adhered to the remaining curved panel of cardstock, which is then glued to the corresponding album-cover panel.

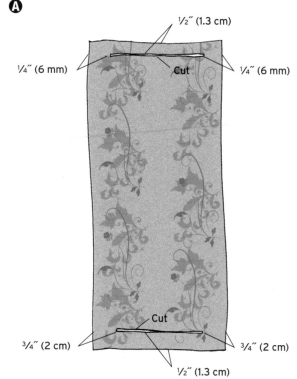

Ⓐ

½″ (1.3 cm)

¼″ (6 mm)   Cut   ¼″ (6 mm)

Cut

¾″ (2 cm)   ¾″ (2 cm)

½″ (1.3 cm)

Connect the Sections

1. Place the portfolio panels on your work surface in the order they will be assembled. Use the center-panel and side-panel templates on pages 126 and 127 to mark the eyelet holes on the corresponding panels; make sure the marks are ⅛" (3 mm) from the edges. Use the curved-panel pattern on page 126 to mark the holes in the remaining panels. Punch ⅛" (3 mm) holes at the marks, and then push an eyelet through each hole. Set the eyelets, using the eyelet tools.

2. Open the jump rings by twisting the ends away from each other to maintain the circle shape, rather than pulling the ends apart. Slip a ring through two corresponding eyelets, and then twist the ring closed. Continue until all the panels are joined. If you use brass jump rings, which are a softer metal, add an extra jump ring in the two middle eyelets of the curved panels and in the three middle eyelets of the side panels to reinforce the hinge.

Make the Closure

1. The portfolio closes by folding in the upper and lower curved panels, and then the right-side panel followed by the left-side panel. Punch a hole large enough to accommodate the doorknob screw on the left panel ½" (1.3 cm) from the edge opposite the jump rings. Push the screw through the hole from the underside. Punch a same-size hole ½" (1.3 cm) from one end of the 30" (76.2 cm) ribbon, push it onto the screw, and then screw on the knob. Wrap the ribbon around the portfolio and secure by wrapping it around the stem of the knob.

TRY THIS

- Portfolios can serve a number of purposes: as a place to showcase artwork and photographs, as an interactive photo album, or as a place to store ephemera.

- Personalize the portfolio as desired, adding pockets, envelopes, or extra flip-up panels.

- Instead of using jump rings, thread narrow ribbon or leather through the eyelets.

Materials

- 10½″ x 5¾″ (26.7 x 15.9 cm) felt rectangle for cover

- 2″ x 2½″ (5.1 x 6.4 cm) felt rectangle for inside pocket

- 10½″ x 5¾″ (26.7 x 15.9 cm) rectangle lightweight cotton fabric for lining

- 10½″ x 5¾″ (26.7 x 15.9 cm) rectangle lightweight double-sided fusible web

- 1″ to 1¼″ (2.5 cm to 3.1 cm) sew-through or shank button for closure

- two ¾″ to ⅞″ (2 cm to 2.2 cm) two-hole sew-through buttons for spine

- twenty-five 7″ x 5¼″ (17.8 x 13.3 cm) sheets text-weight paper, folded in half (Set aside one folio for signature-punching template, and group remaining into six signatures of four folios each.)

- 60″ (1.83 m) piece of waxed linen thread

- 12″ (30.5 cm) piece of waxed linen thread

- bookbinding needle

- needle and sewing thread in a contrasting color to felt

- straight pins

- repositionable low-tack tape

- optional decorations: embroidery thread, felt and fabric scraps, beads, pearls, sequins, small shells

- cover-punching template (page 128)

- signature-punching template (page 127)

- cardstock for copying templates

Felted Sweater Journal

BINDING STYLE: **LONG STITCH** | APPROXIMATE FINISHED SIZE: 4″ x 5 ³/₄″ (10.2 x 14.6 cm)

When wool sweaters, scarves, and skirts have outlived their appeal or been snacked on by moths, give them a new life by turning them into take-along journals. To make the transformation, the wool must first be felted, a washing process that tightly binds the fibers, making the fabric thick, durable, and fray-free. These covers look terrific plain (especially if using a patterned wool) or decorated with embroidery and beading. Felted wool is usually heavy enough to forgo using an embroidery hoop when embellishing.

Choose items made of 100 percent wool. Even a small amount of synthetic or natural fibers blended with the wool may prevent the wool from felting. Avoid articles labeled "superwash" or that have machine washing and drying instructions, as the wool has been specially treated not to felt. To felt wool, set the machine for heavy-duty agitation with a hot-water wash and cold rinse, and add a tablespoon of gentle detergent. Place the garment in a mesh laundry bag and set it in the machine. Garments can also be placed in a zippered pillowcase to reduce the amount of fibers produced, which can clog the machine. Adding a pair of jeans to the load will increase friction and hasten the felting. Agitate for ten minutes, and check the felting. If you want the piece felted more, reset the timer for another five minutes, and then check again. Reset the machine for another five minutes if desired. If the wool doesn't felt within twenty minutes, it isn't going to. Either air- or machine-dry the felt; machine drying sometimes results in a fuzzy texture.

The long-stitch binding sews the signatures directly to the cover. The structure opens flat, and there is plenty of room to add photos or ephemera.

TIP
Those used to making exact measurements with paper and book board may find working with fabric a bit frustrating, since the process isn't as precise. Don't worry—the imperfections only add to the appeal and beauty of the book.

41

Make the Cover

1. To determine the placement of cover embellishments, stack the signatures together to form the text block, and then place the text block on the cover felt piece 3¾″ (9.5 cm) from the left edge. Wrap the felt around the text block so the felt left edge is flush with the text block fore edge, and the felt right edge overlaps the left edge, creating the front-closure flap. With needle and thread, baste the cover's upper and lower edges at the following locations: on the underneath layer where the flap ends, on the flap where it overlaps the front cover fore edge, on the buttonhole, and on either side of the spine **(A)**.

2. Sew a blanket stitch around the perimeter of the cover, and then decorate the cover with any combination of embroidery, felt or fabric scraps, beads, buttons, sequins, and small shells. Leave the spine plain so the signatures can be easily sewn.

3. With wrong sides together, attach the cotton fabric to the inside cover with fusible web following the manufacturer's instructions.

4. With the inside of the cover facing up, measure 3¾″ (9.5 cm) from the left edge and mark with a pin. Copy the cover-punching template on page 128 onto cardstock and cut out. Line up the left edge of the template with the pin, and secure the template to the fabric with low-tack tape **(B)**. Punch the holes with an awl or a screw punch fitted with a 1-mm tip. If the holes are difficult to see, mark them on the inside cover with a pen or marker. The marks won't show once the book is bound.

A

Basting stitches

Baste-mark cover for embellishment placement.

B

3 ¾″ (9.5 cm)

Inside view of cover

Template

Position cover-punching template inside the cover.

TIP
Felt is easily and neatly cut with a rotary cutter. When cutting, don't toss details such as ribbing, buttonholes, and pockets—they can be incorporated into the design.

TRY THIS
- Not into embroidery? Fuse felt or fabric scraps to the cover.
- Substitute one or more rows of crochet stitches for the blanket stitch around the edge of the book.
- Use the felt to make a cover for a Moleskine or other premade journal.

Sew the Book

1. Use the signature-punching guide on page 127 to mark the single folio to create the signature-punching template. Use the template to punch holes in the signatures.

2. Thread the bookbinding needle with the 60″ (1.5 m) waxed linen thread. Enter the cover and the first signature from the outside through the top hole of the right row, leaving a 10″ (25.4 cm) tail. Working down the row, exit the next hole from the inside, enter the next hole from the outside, and then exit the last hole from the inside, forming a running stitch. Go directly across to the next row of holes, enter from the outside, and pick up the second signature. Sew the second signature with the same in-and-out running stitches, and then go across to the next row and pick up the third signature. Continue until all six signatures are sewn, and the thread is outside the cover at the top (C).

3. Take the needle back through the upper holes of the previous two rows, sewing only through the cover layer—do not go into the signatures. Enter the top hole of the fifth signature, and then exit the top hole of the fourth signature. Remove the needle and rethread it with the tail at the first signature. Reverse the sewing pattern, going in and out of the top holes in the second and third signatures. Thread a needle with the 12″ (30.5 cm) waxed linen thread. Enter the bottom hole of the fourth signature, and then exit through the bottom hole of the third signature; even out the thread ends (D). All thread ends should be outside the cover.

4. Lace both upper threads through a button and pull the ends, snugging the button to the spine. Tie a square knot underneath the button and trim the ends. Attach a button to the lower threads in the same manner (E).

5. Use a craft knife or chisel, and cut a buttonhole through the cover flap and lining large enough to accommodate the closure button. Blanket stitch around the slit. Attach the button to the front cover directly underneath the buttonhole.

6. For the pocket, embellish the remaining small felt rectangle if desired. Attach the pocket to the inside of the front cover with a blanket stitch.

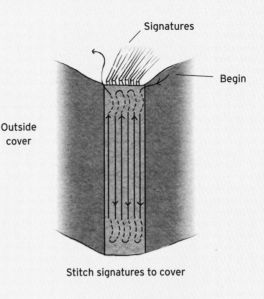

C

Signatures

Begin

Outside cover

Stitch signatures to cover

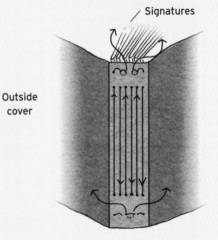

D

Signatures

Outside cover

Prepare thread ends for attaching bottoms.

E

Attach buttons with thread ends.

Cabinet-Card Sketchbook

BINDING STYLE: STAB BINDING | APPROXIMATE FINISHED SIZE: 4 ¼″ x 6 ½″ (10.8 x 16.5 cm)

Cabinet cards are irresistible collectibles. These beautiful portraits, which became popular in the mid-to late nineteenth century, feature individuals, families, and sometimes animals. The photographs were glued to chipboard or heavyweight cardstock, which makes them ideal for book covers. Here, cabinet cards are turned into a double-sided book that's both attractive and practical—one side for sketching, the other for note taking. The removable books slip easily out of the sleeve pockets, so the cover can be used again and again.

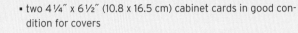

Materials

- two 4 ¼″ x 6 ½″ (10.8 x 16.5 cm) cabinet cards in good condition for covers
- cabinet card for spine (See "Prepare the Covers," step 1, on page 48 for exact sizing.)
- forty 6″ x 3 ¾″ (15.2 x 9.5 cm) sheets text-weight paper, grain short (Amount may be adjusted; pages should be about ¼″ [6 mm] thick when stacked together.)
- forty 6″ x 3 ¾″ (15.2 x 9.5 cm) sheets lightweight drawing paper, grain short (Amount may be adjusted; pages should be about ¼″ [6 mm] thick when stacked together.)
- two 6″ x 3 ¾″ (15.2 x 9.5 cm) lightweight chipboard rectangles for sketchbook and notebook backing
- two 6″ x 3 ¾″ (15.2 x 9.5 cm) decorative cardstock rectangles, grain short, for sketchbook and notebook covers
- two 5″ x 6″ (12.7 x 15.2 cm) cardstock rectangles for sleeves (should closely match cabinet card reverse sides)
- two 42″ (104 cm) lengths of ⅛″ (3 mm) -wide double-face satin ribbon to bind cover
- two 24″ (61 cm) lengths of ⅛″ (3 mm) -wide double-face satin ribbon to bind sketchbook and notebook
- two 9″ (22.9 cm) lengths of ½″ to ¾″ (1.3 to 2 cm) -wide ribbon for closure
- PVA or strong double-stick tape
- super glue
- two tapestry needles (optional)
- binder clips
- signature-punching template (page 129)
- cover-punching template (page 130)
- spine-punching template (page 130)

Prepare the Sketchbook and Notebook

1. Use the signature-punching template on page 129 to mark the holes on each 6″ x 3¾″ (15.2 x 9.5 cm) decorative cardstock rectangle. Assemble the following in order for both books: decorative cardstock cover, pages, and chipboard; hold each group together with a binder clip. Punch holes through all layers using a rotary or an electric drill. For neater holes, drill from the chipboard side with the electric dill, and from the cardstock side with the rotary drill. The pages will expand after being drilled; simply pinch them back together. Do not remove the binder clips.

2. Thread a tapestry needle with a 24″ (61 cm) ribbon. Pick up the sketchbook, and insert the needle from back to front through the bottom hole, leaving a 3″ (7.6 cm) tail. Stitch the subsequent holes toward the top, always working from back to front, without twisting the ribbon, and keeping the ribbon taut. At the top hole, wrap the ribbon to the back of the text block, and then enter the same hole, from back to front, being careful not to split the ribbon with the needle (A). Stitch back down through the holes, this time working from front to back, and ending on the front. At the bottom hole, wrap the ribbon around the text block, and tie a square knot at the back of the bottom hole (B). Trim the ends to about ¼″ (6 mm), and then secure with a drop of super glue. Remove the binder clip. Repeat for the other notebook.

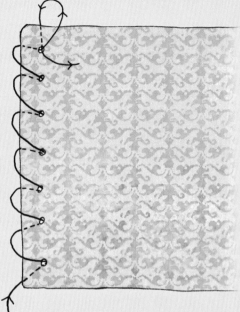

Stitch, wrapping ribbon around edges.

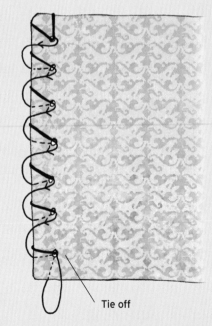

Tie off

Stitch in opposite direction; tie off.

Prepare the Sleeves

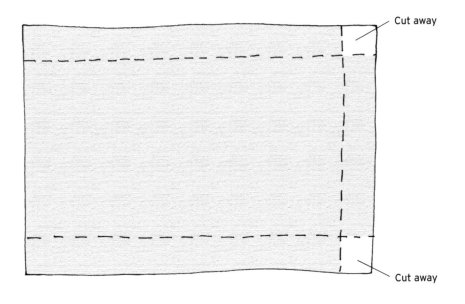

Score and fold dashed lines.

Cut away

Cut away

1. For the notebook and sketchbook sleeves, score and fold the 5″ x 6″ (12.7 x 15.2 cm) cardstock rectangles ½″ (1.3 cm) from both long edges and one short edge. Cut out the two ½″ (1.3 cm) squares created by the folds at the corners **(C)**. Fold in the long sides, and then the short side. Secure the overlapping corners together with PVA or double-stick tape **(D)**.

TRY THIS

- **For a masculine-looking book, bind the covers with hemp or suede laces. Instead of a ribbon closure, use leather strips or frayed fabric strips.**
- **To permanently adhere the sketchbook and notebook to the covers, eliminate the sleeves and glue or tape the back cover of each directly to the inside of the cabinet-card covers.**
- **Use heavyweight vintage bingo cards for covers instead of cabinet cards.**

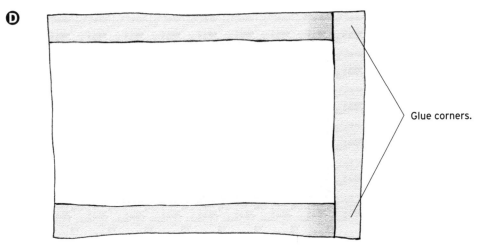

Glue corners.

Prepare the Covers

1. To make an accurate measurement for the spine, assemble the following in order: one cabinet-card cover, sketchbook sleeve, sketchbook, notebook, notebook sleeve, and cabinet card cover. The width between the cabinet cards equals the spine width. Cut the remaining cabinet card to the determined width by 6 ½˝ (16.5 cm) tall.

2. Decide which cabinet card will be the front and back cover. Use the cover-punching template on page 130 to punch ⅛˝ (3 mm) holes on each cover along the edge to be joined to the spine. Use the spine-punching template on page 130 to punch ⅛˝ (3 mm) holes along both long sides of the spine.

3. Sew the covers to the spine using two tapestry needles, or simply thread the ribbon through the holes. For the latter, trim the ribbon ends at an angle to help ease them through the holes, and coat with a thin layer of glue; let dry. Sew the front cover to the spine by bringing both ends of the 42˝ (12.8 cm) ribbon through the top two holes from the inside; pull the ribbon ends even. Cross the ribbons and enter the next two holes from the outside. Cross the ribbons and exit out the same holes with the opposite ribbons (E). Make sure the ribbons lie flat.

(As you join the sections, make sure the cabinet-card edges are just touching. If the cards overlap, the covers won't close properly, and if they're too far apart, the covers will be loose.) Cross the ribbons and enter the next two holes from the outside, cross the ribbons, and then exit the same two holes. Continue in this pattern until the last cross has been made on the outside, and both ribbon ends are inside the cover. Tie the ends in a square knot, trim to ¼˝ (6 mm), and secure with a drop of super glue. Repeat to sew the back cover to the spine. When finished, there should be a neat row of Xs down both sides of the spine (F).

4. With a craft knife cut a slit ½˝ (1.3 cm) from and centered along the fore edge of the front and back covers. Make the slit equal to the closure-ribbon width. Push the ribbon ½˝ (1.3 cm) through the slit to the inside; secure the end with PVA (G).

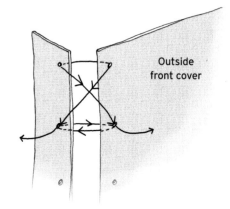

E

Begin sewing binding from inside covers.

F

Ribbons form X's on spine

G

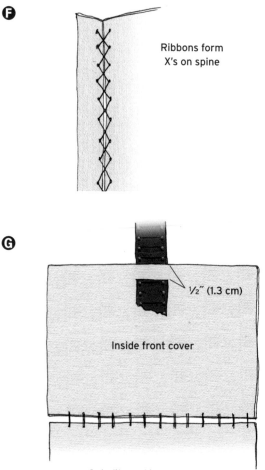

½˝ (1.3 cm)

Inside front cover

Cut slits and insert ribbons.

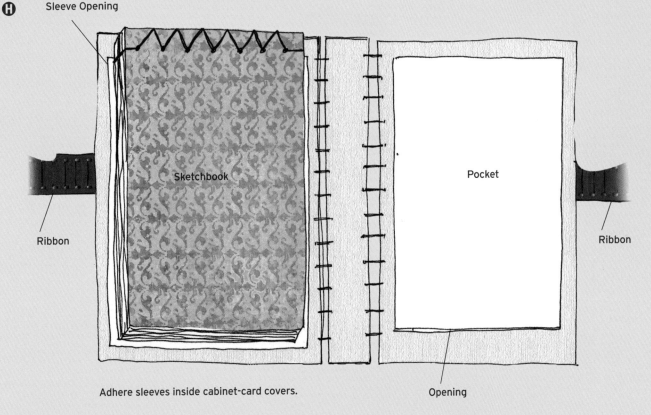

H

Sleeve Opening

Sketchbook

Ribbon

Pocket

Ribbon

Adhere sleeves inside cabinet-card covers.

Opening

Assemble the Book

1. Slip the back cover of the sketchbook into a sleeve and place it on the inside of one cover with the sketchbook binding at the top (this can be reversed for left-handed users). The sleeve should not overlap the cover binding. Lightly mark the sleeve placement with a pencil. Remove the sketchbook from the sleeve, apply glue or attach double-stick tape to the sleeve flaps, and then adhere the sleeve to the inside of the cover **(H)**. Do the same with the notebook and notebook sleeve. Slide the sketchbook and notebook into their sleeves, and tie the book closed with the ribbons.

TIPS
- Decorate the covers with two-dimensional embellishments so the book will lie flat when open, making it easier to draw and write.
- If the slits for the ribbons look messy, cover them with a flower, or a piece of fabric, lace, or decorative paper.

CHAPTER 4

From Mundane to Marvelous: Hardware, Home Supply, and Office Supply Stores

Hardware and office supply stores may not be the first places that come to mind when searching for book elements, but they can provide a wealth of materials and infinite possibilities for very little money.

Cruise the aisles with the mind of a book artist. When looking for cover materials, scope out items that are relatively flat and sturdy, and could, if necessary, be drilled or punched to create holes for sewing or attaching embellishments. At hardware and home supply stores, switch-plate covers can become mini books—the opening is perfect for framing a photograph or quotation. Eye-catching graphics on metal and plastic signs make ideal covers for photo albums and journals. Window screen and chicken wire door mesh come in a variety of sizes, and all work as book covers and spines. Use artificial grass to make a garden journal. And don't forget to peruse the scrap bin for ¼" (6 mm) -thick plywood.

At office supply stores, consider file dividers and file folders, which can be cut into any shape or used as is for covers. Try sewing pages directly into the crease of a file folder using an easy three- or five-hole pamphlet stitch for an ultra-quick book (for pamphlet-stitch instructions, see "Game-Board Travel Journal, Make the Accordion," step 4 on page 79). Punch holes in CD edges and link them together for an unconventional accordion structure. Colorful plastic pouches bend enough to be used as wraparound journal covers. Or how about thick cork sheets for covers, to which you can tack a note?

Smaller elements can be used for the binding or as decoration. Hardware store hinges come in a variety of sizes, shapes, and metals, as do bolts, screws, and washers. Drawer pulls and knobs make terrific book handles, or you can shape metal strapping into a handle. Rubber washers come in different colors and add a softer element. Various gauges and types of wire can be used for binding as well as fastening embellishments. When working with metal, consider making a small investment in wire cutters, tin snips, and a metal file to make the job easier.

Office supply stores are packed with usable elements such as tags, binder clips, paper clips, and rubber bands. Ideas abound for nontraditional text pages: graph and notebook paper, receipt and ledger books, index cards, and envelopes.

Hardware store books in this chapter include a photo album with a paint-chip cover and brass hinge, and a house-shaped art journal made from window screen with the signatures sewn directly to the spine. Envelopes available from the office supply store become a twelve-month organizer with pockets attached to an accordion fold. Strips of tickets are woven to form the covers for a simple one-signature mini book.

Paint-Sample Photo Album

BINDING STYLE: **HINGED AND BOLTED BINDING** | APPROXIMATE FINISHED SIZE: 9 ¾″ x 3″ (24.8 x 7.6 cm)

Almost every element of this album comes from the hardware store. It goes together easily and requires no sewing, making it ideal for quick gifts. A double layer of cardstock on the left side of the album allows for adding photographs and embellishments that won't cause the book to swell.

Materials

- four 10″ x 3″ (25.4 x 7.6 cm) paint-chip samples in desired colors
- ten 11″ x 3″ (27.9 x 7.6 cm) sheets cardstock for pages, grain short
- two ½″ (1.3 cm) ¼-20 brass hex-head bolts
- two ¼ flat brass washers
- two ¼-20 brass acorn nuts
- ¾″ x 2″ (1.9 x 5.1 cm) brass hinge (may be up to 1″ x 2″ [2.5 x 5.1 cm])
- eyelets to fit holes in brass hinge (number of eyelets may vary depending on hinge), eyelet-setting tools
- 1 ⅝″ (5.1 cm) rubber O-ring
- PVA
- super glue
- ¼″ (6 mm) hole punch

TIPS

- This album can be adapted to various sizes of paint samples. Inside pages should be cut the same height as the sample. To determine the page width, measure the width of the paint sample, and add 1″ (2.5 cm). Score the pages at 1¼″ and 2¾″ (3 cm and 7 cm) from the left short side. After punching the holes, cut the cover 1½″ (3.8 cm) from the left side. Affix an appropriately sized hinge, and assemble the book with bolts.
- If adding extra pages or embellishments inside the album, use longer hex-head bolts.

Photographs by Andrea Stein

Joey & Michael • August 2008

Dipped in Honey
A23-2

Assemble the Book

1. Determine the paint samples to be used for the front and back covers. With wrong sides facing, glue another paint chip to each cover with PVA. If the paint samples resist the glue, press them under a heavy weight for about ten minutes.

2. While the glue dries, prepare the inside pages. Measure and score each page at 1 ¼˝ and 2 ¾˝ (3 cm and 7 cm) from the left short end **(A)**. Fold each page back at the 1 ¼˝ (3 cm) mark. Round all corners, except for the ends folded back **(B)**.

3. On the left end of the front cover, mark two points ½˝ (1.3 cm) in from the end and ½˝ (1.3 cm) from the upper and lower edges **(C)**. Sandwich the inside pages between the covers, with the pages flush with the marked end. Punch ¼˝ (6 mm) holes through the covers and pages at the two points.

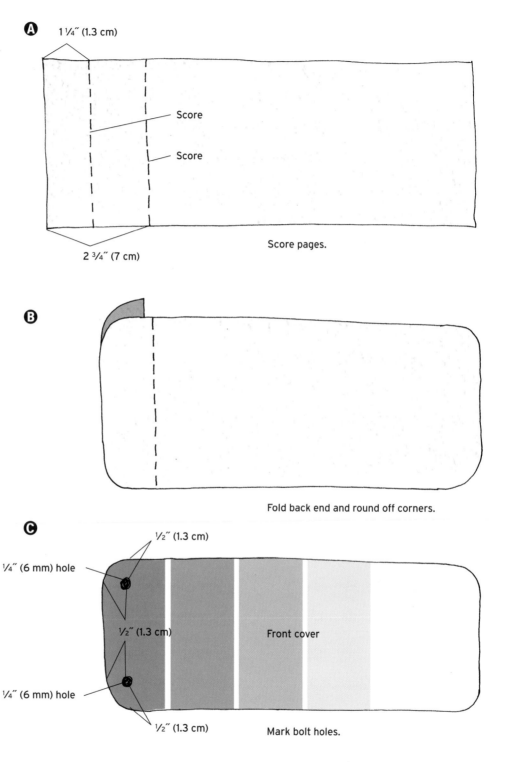

Ⓐ 1 ¼˝ (1.3 cm)

Score

Score

2 ¾˝ (7 cm)

Score pages.

Ⓑ

Fold back end and round off corners.

Ⓒ ½˝ (1.3 cm)

¼˝ (6 mm) hole

½˝ (1.3 cm)

Front cover

¼˝ (6 mm) hole

½˝ (1.3 cm)

Mark bolt holes.

4. Remove the cover and measure 1 ½″ (3.8 cm) from the drilled end. Cut the cover into two sections with a craft knife **(D)**. Place the left side of the hinge on the smaller cover section, making sure the hinge center is directly over the cut; mark the eyelet positions and punch the holes. Set the eyelets (see "Twelve-month Organizer, Make the Closure, " on page 67) to secure the hinge. Place the larger cover piece under the right side of the hinge, butting it up against the smaller cover piece. Mark and punch holes, and then set the eyelets **(E)**.

5. Place the pages between the covers and align the holes. Insert the bolts from the back, place the washers over the bolts, and then screw on the acorn nuts **(F)**. Use the O-ring as a photo frame on the cover. Glue the photo to the back of the O-ring and then adhere the ring with super glue.

D

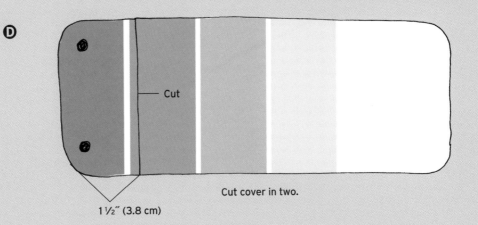

Cut

1 ½″ (3.8 cm)

Cut cover in two.

E

Join hinge to cover pieces with eyelets.

TRY THIS
- Substitute wing nuts for the acorn nuts.
- For another look, use screw posts instead of the hex-head bolts, and replace brass washers with rubber washers, which come in a variety of colors.

F

Acorn nut

Washer

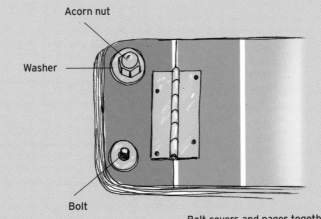

Bolt

Bolt covers and pages together

Window-Screen Art Journal

BINDING STYLE: LINK STITCH
APPROXIMATE FINISHED SIZE: 5″ x 11″ (12.7 x 27.9 cm)

Window screen may be utilitarian, but in the hands of a book artist it becomes an intriguing and sturdy see-through cover for a house-shaped art journal. Hardware appears in the handle and hinges, and a treasured photo is framed by a switch-plate covered with vintage wallpaper. Hard edges are softened with fabric, making the book inviting to touch, and the peaked pages offer endless possibilities for decorating and writing. Because of the book's heft, it's a good idea to decorate the pages as desired before binding. Signatures are sewn with a simple link stitch that connects to the screen. This is a book that commands center stage on a coffee table or display shelf.

Materials

- 15″ (38.1 cm) square of ¼″ (6 mm) -grid aluminum window screen
- four 1 ½″ x 7 ⅜″ (3.8 x 18.8 cm) fabric scraps for covers
- six 1 ½″ x 5″ (3.8 x 12.7 cm) fabric scraps for covers
- sixteen 9 ¾″ x 10 ¾″ (24.7 x 27.3 cm) cardstock rectangles, grain long
- seventeen 9 ¾″ x 7 ¾″ (24.7 x 18.8 cm) cardstock rectangles, grain short, folded in half widthwise
- two 48″ (1.2 m) lengths of 20-lb. hemp cord
- beeswax
- 4 tapestry needles
- four 10″ (25.4 cm) lengths of ⅜″ (1 cm) -wide velvet ribbon for hinges
- eight 8-32 brass hex nuts for hinges
- thick craft glue and PVA
- 2 ⅞″ x 4 ⅝″ (7.3 x 11.8 cm) dimmer-switch plate, plastic or metal
- 4″ x 5 ¾″ (10.2 x 14.6 cm) rectangle vintage wallpaper for dimmer switch
- 2 ⅝″ x 4 ⅜″ (6.7 x 11.2 cm) rectangle vintage wallpaper for dimmer switch
- wire cutters
- heavy-duty awl
- flat bastard metal file
- copper tube strap for handle
- two ¼″ (6 mm) 6-32 brass machine screws for handle
- two 6-32 brass acorn nuts for handle
- plastic mirror rosette
- protective gloves, goggles, and dust mask
- 24-gauge annealed wire
- low-tack artist, painter's, or masking tape
- strong double-sided tape
- scraps of decorative trim, lace, and ribbon
- small vintage key
- trim pattern (page 131)
- folio pattern (page 131)
- photograph

Prepare the Covers

1. Wear protective gloves and goggles when handling the metal screen. Flatten the screen with your hands if it is curled or warped. Window-screen squares do not measure the same horizontally and vertically. For this project, use the direction where 20 squares equal 5″ (12.7 cm) for the shorter measurements. Cut the screen with wire cutters as close to the square edges as possible.

2. For the covers, cut two 5″ x 11″ (12.7 x 27.9 cm) rectangles (20 squares by 43 squares). To cut the peaks, align tape with the center of the 5″ (12.7 cm) edge and the bottom of the 14th square from the edge **(A)**. Do the same for the other side of the peak. Use the tape edges as a cutting guide, and cut the screen with wire cutters.

3. For the spine, cut a 1¼″ x 7⅜″ (3 x 18.8 cm) screen strip (5 squares by 29 squares). The spine won't have a fabric border, so the edges must be filed smooth with a flat bastard file. Wear goggles and a dust mask, and file away from you—don't move the file back and forth.

4. Create ⅛″ (3 mm) fringe on the fabric strips by pulling a few threads from the long edges. Apply a thick layer of craft glue to the fabric wrong side, on the lengthwise half of the longer 1½″ (3.8 cm) -wide strips, and then fold the strips around the long sides of both covers; hold in place until the glue adheres **(B)**. Glue a shorter 1½″ (3.8 cm) -wide fabric strip around each cover's lower edge. Copy the trim pattern on page 131 and use it to shape the remaining 1½″ (3.8 cm) -wide strips, and then glue one to each side of the peaks; allow the glue to dry.

A

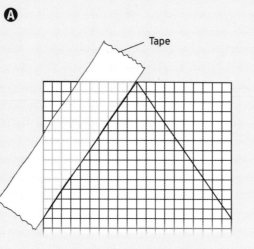

Apply tape for cutting guide.

B

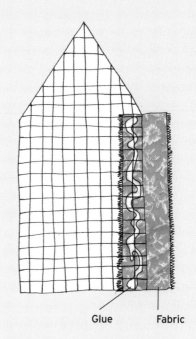

Wrap screen edges with fabric.

C

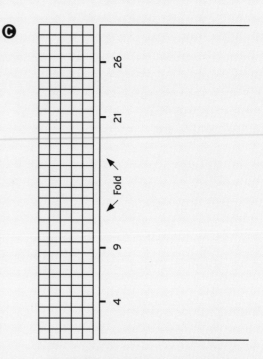

Align template with spine and mark holes.

Prepare the Signatures

1. Photocopy the folio pattern on page 131 at 200 percent; cut out the pattern. Fold the sixteen larger cardstock rectangles in half to form 4 7/8″ x 10 3/4″ (12.4 x 27.3 cm) rectangles; cut the peaks using the pattern. Fold the remaining cardstock pages to form 4 7/8″ x 7 3/8″ (12.4 x 18.8 cm) rectangles. Assemble a signature by nesting the folded pages in this order: peaked page, short page, peaked page, and short page. Repeat to form seven more signatures. Use the extra short page as the signature-punching template. Align the template's folded edge alongside the spine and mark the hole placement as follows: at the center of the 4th, 9th, 21st, and 26th squares (C). Insert the template inside each signature, align the folds, and then punch the holes with an awl.

Sew the Text Block

1. This binding is sewn across the spine with two needles and one thread. Pull a 48″ (1.2 m) length of hemp cord through beeswax two or three times. Thread a needle onto each end of the cord. Pick up the first signature. From inside the signature insert one needle in the hole closest to the tail, and insert the other needle in the neighboring hole; exit through the spine's first column in rows #4 and #9. (D). Even out the thread ends. The lower two holes of the remaining signatures are sewn across the spine also in rows #4 and #9. Pick up the second signature and place it next to the first. Pass over the screen grid and insert the needles in the spine's second column and into the second signature (E). Cross threads on the inside and exit, making sure not to split the threads (F). Tighten the threads by pulling them toward the head and tail of the spine; tighten the threads each time they are outside of the signatures.

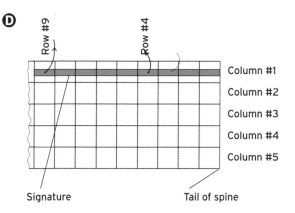

Enter two lower holes of first signature; exit through spine.

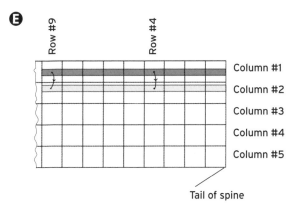

Cross over screen and enter second signature.

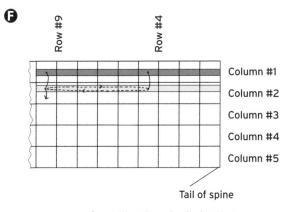

Cross threads and exit signature.

2. Pick up the third signature and enter both holes, staying in the second column of the spine. Cross the threads on the inside and exit through the spine **(G)**.

3. Cross over the screen, enter the third column, pick up the fourth signature, and enter both holes; cross the threads on the inside and exit. Pick up the fifth signature, enter both holes, staying in the third column; cross the threads on the inside and exit **(H)**.

4. Pick up and stitch the sixth and seventh signatures in the same manner in the spine's fourth column. Cross over the screen into the fifth column, pick up the eighth signature, and enter both holes. Tie the threads inside the signature with a square knot, and then trim the ends to ¼" (6 mm) **(I)**.

5. Stitch the upper two holes of each signature to the spine in the same manner, working across the spine in rows #21 and #26.

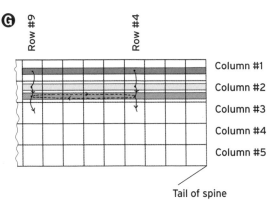

Sew third signature, staying in second column.

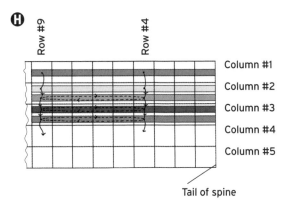

Sew fourth and fifth signatures in third column.

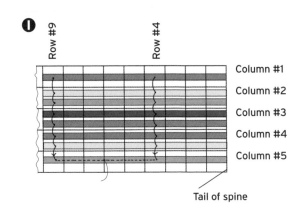

Attach last signature and tie off.

Hinge the Book Together

1. Lace the four 10" (25.4 cm) velvet ribbons across the spine at the 2nd, 12th, 18th, and 28th rows. Lace each ribbon under the first vertical grid, across the spine, and then under the last vertical grid **(J)**. Even out the ribbon ends.

2. Place the front cover over the text block and align it with the spine. Use the awl to punch holes through the fabric close to the edge that abuts the spine and is directly across from the ribbons. Lace each ribbon through its corresponding hole from the underside. Slip a hex nut onto each ribbon **(K)**, and then tie an overhand knot close to the nut. Turn the book over and join the back cover in the same manner. Trim the ribbon ends.

TIP

- Shiny metal can take on a vintage look with patinas. Give copper an antique finish by dipping it into liver-of-sulfur solution, following the manufacturer's instructions. Or add color by heating the metal over an open flame or with a heat-embossing tool (found in craft stores), bringing out an array of colors from gold to violet. Darken brass with brass-aging solution, or try other patina solutions made for metal.

J

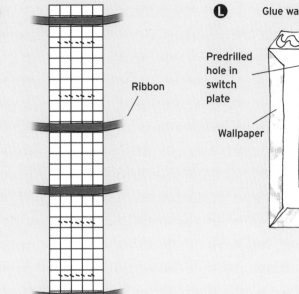

Ribbon

Lace ribbons through spine.

K

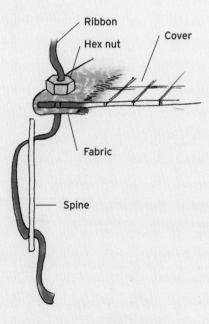

Ribbon

Hex nut

Cover

Fabric

Spine

Join covers to spine and secure ribbons with hex nuts.

L

Glue wallpaper to switch plate.

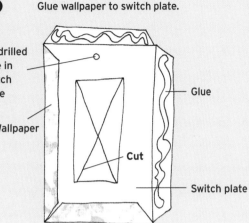

Predrilled hole in switch plate

Wallpaper

Glue

Cut

Switch plate

Cover the Switch Plate

1. Apply PVA to the front of the switch plate, center the switch plate over the wrong side of the larger wallpaper rectangle, and smooth in place. Trim the wallpaper diagonally across the corners, leaving a generous 1/8″ (3 mm). Apply glue to the overhanging edges and adhere to the underside of the switch plate. Use a craft knife to cut an X in the switch-plate opening **(L)**. Turn in and glue each triangle to the underside of the switch plate, trimming the triangle points as needed so they don't extend past the switch-plate edge.

2. Adhere a photograph to the switch plate with strong double-stick tape, and then glue the smaller wallpaper rectangle to the back.

3. Use an awl to pierce through the wallpaper at the small switch-plate holes.

Finish the Book

1. Mark through the copper-strap holes onto the fabric of the front-cover fore edge; punch the fabric with a heavy-duty awl. Attach the copper strap with two 1/4″ (6 mm) machine screws and acorn nuts.

2. Thread ribbon through the front cover, and then through the upper hole of the switch-plate frame; tie the ribbon in a knot. Tie the lower frame to the front cover in the same manner, adding a plastic mirror rosette to the ribbon before tying the knot. (Fabric scraps, hemp cord, or annealed wire can also be used to attach the frame.)

3. Attach the key with wire to the front-cover peak. Cover areas where the edge fabrics meet with decorative trim or lace.

TRY THIS

- Metal screen comes in array of styles; experiment with different types for a variety of looks.
- Take advantage of the grid to try various hinging and binding styles, plus add washers or beads along the spine.
- Almost anything can be attached to the screen for decoration. If you tire of an embellishment, change it, making the book a dynamic work of art.

Twelve-Month Organizer

BINDING STYLE: **DOUBLE ACCORDION BINDING WITH GATEFOLD COVER**
APPROXIMATE FINISHED SIZE: **11 ½" x 6 ¼" (29.2 x 15.8 cm)**

Yearly organizers are often generic and uninteresting, but this utilitarian item doesn't have to be dull. Decorate heavy file dividers, file folders, and kraft envelopes, and then transform them into a unique organizer that's stylish and suits your needs. When creating an accordion binding, go slowly and make sure the folds are even and neat, resulting in a sturdier book. A bone folder is an absolute necessity for making crisp, clean folds.

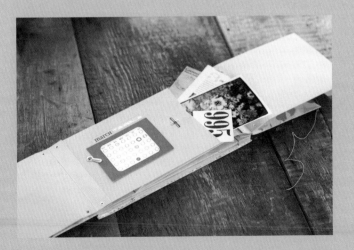

Materials

- 3 heavyweight, three-tab, letter-size file dividers for the front and back covers (Two file dividers should have center tabs. Pendaflex brand was used for this project.)
- two rectangles 18" x 6" (45.7 x 15.2 cm) heavyweight card-stock, grain short, for the accordion binding
- twelve 6" x 9" (15.2 x 22.9 cm) kraft envelopes with clasp
- twelve 6" x 2" (15.2 x 5.1 cm) decorative-paper rectangles for envelope-flap linings
- 11 ½" x 6 ¼" (29.2 x 15.8 cm) decorative-paper rectangle for back-cover lining
- two 6 ¼" (15.8 cm) decorative-paper squares for front-cover lining
- four ⅜" x 5" (1 x 12.7 cm) strips cut from plastic folder for front and back covers
- twenty-two ⅛" (3 mm) eyelets, eyelet-setting tools
- two ¾" (1.9 cm) -diameter circles cut from plastic folder
- letter-size file folders
- 12 photo turns
- 12 miniature brads
- glue stick
- PVA
- ¼" (6 mm) hole punch
- ⅛" (3 mm) hole punch, or Japanese screw punch with 2.5-mm tip
- ¾" (1.9 cm) circle punch (found in scrapbook section of craft stores)
- double-stick tape
- repositionable low-tack tape
- 16" (40.6 cm) waxed linen thread for closure
- decorative rubber stamps (optional)
- permanent stamping ink (optional)
- hammer
- cardstock for printing calendars

Prepare the Covers

1. Cut two front-cover panels from the letter-size file dividers with center tabs, being as precise as possible to ensure that the covers will interlock when closed **(A)**. If the specified file dividers are unavailable, cut two 5 ⅞" x 6 ¼" (14.9 x 15.8 cm) rectangles from the dividers to make a gatefold cover that will not interlock. Cut an 11 ¾" x 6 ¼" (29.8 x 15.8 cm) rectangle from the remaining divider for the back cover.

2. If desired, decorate the front and back covers using decorative rubber stamps. Try various types of permanent inks on a scrap piece of file divider to see which work best.

Prepare the Envelopes

1. The envelope adhesive may become sticky in humid weather, so the inside flaps are covered with paper. Apply glue stick to the underside of one envelope flap and adhere a 6" x 2" (15.2 x 5.1 cm) piece of decorative paper. Place the paper next to the fold, and then trim away the excess, following the flap edge. Re-punch the flap hole in the decorative paper with a ¼" (6 mm) hole punch. Repeat for the remaining eleven envelopes.

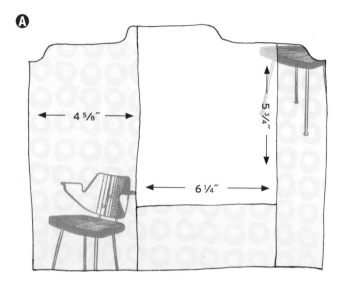

A

4 ⅝"

5 ¾"

6 ¼"

Cut the front covers.

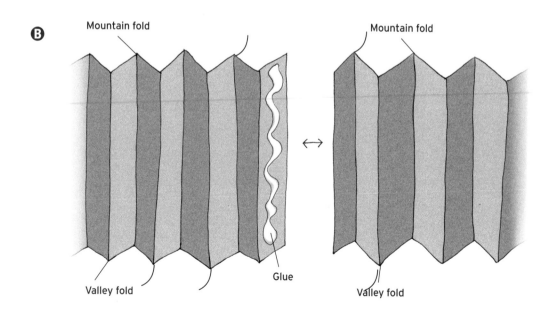

B

Mountain fold

Mountain fold

Glue

Valley fold

Valley fold

↔

Join two sections if necessary for accordion.

Make the Accordion Bindings

1. Make seventeen 1″ (2.5 cm) marks along the upper and lower edges of both 18″ (45.7 cm) -long pieces of heavyweight cardstock, beginning 1″ (2.5 cm) from the short edge and spacing them 1″ (2.5 cm) apart. Align a ruler with the marks, score the lines, and then accordion fold, making sure the folds are aligned. If the rectangles cannot be cut from one sheet of cardstock, join the folded pieces by gluing one side of a valley fold to one side of a mountain fold to create one continuous piece **(B)**.

2. Position one accordion on your work surface so it begins and ends with a valley fold. Place a small piece of double-stick tape on the first side of the adjoining mountain fold and adhere an envelope, making sure the envelope flap faces toward the accordion center. Collapse the mountain fold, mark the eyelet positions ¼″ (6 mm) from each edge, and centered between the folds. Punch through both sides of the fold and the envelope with a ⅛″ (3 mm) hole punch or a Japanese screw punch. Insert an eyelet through the fold holes and then through the envelope **(C)**. Position the accordion and envelope on a hard surface, such as a cutting mat, insert an eyelet setter into the eyelet unfinished end, and then hammer the setter until the eyelet flattens out **(D)**.

TIPS

- To find the center of a circle, cut a same-size circle from scrap paper, fold it in half, and then in half again. The intersection of the two folds is the center. Use the scrap paper circle as a template for punching holes in other circles.
- Don't settle for boring paper clips, binder clips, and file folders. Office-supply stores have gotten savvy, offering utilitarian items in chic, sophisticated patterns and colors.

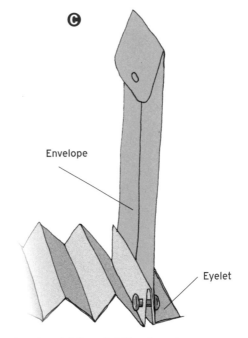

C

Envelope

Eyelet

Insert eyelet through fold and envelope.

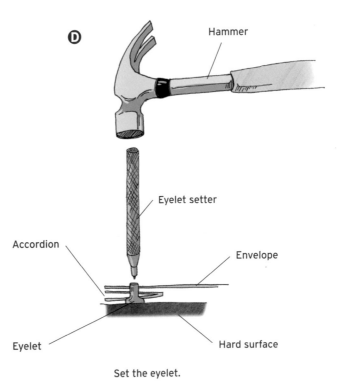

D

Hammer

Eyelet setter

Accordion

Envelope

Eyelet

Hard surface

Set the eyelet.

3. Adhere an envelope to the next mountain fold in the same way. Join the third set of mountain folds together with eyelets, but eliminate the envelope. This gives the book extra expansion room as the envelopes are filled. Adhere two more envelopes to the next two mountain folds, join just a mountain fold, then adhere two more envelopes to mountain folds. There should be one flap remaining **(E)**. Repeat for the other accordion and six remaining envelopes.

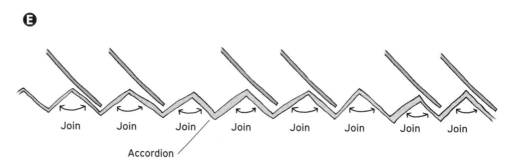

Join 6 envelopes to accordion.

Assemble the Book

1. Apply PVA to the underside of the last flap of one accordion, and then adhere it to the inside of the back cover with the accordion fold flush with the shorter cover edge—make sure the envelope flaps face outward. Repeat with the other accordion, making sure the envelope flaps face in the opposite direction **(F)**.

2. Apply PVA to the back of the 11 ½″ x 6 ¼″ (29.2 x 15.8 cm) rectangle of decorative paper and adhere it to the inside back cover, covering the accordion flaps.

3. Place the front covers faceup on a flat surface with the tabs interlocked, and the total width is 11 ¾″ (29.8 cm). Secure the covers together with repositionable low-tack tape to ensure the covers interlock properly. (If making a non-interlocking gatefold, position both

covers so they abut, and secure with repositionable tape.) Position the cover over the book and make sure it fits, is centered, and is even. Remove the cover.

4. Slip a piece of scrap paper under each accordion flap to protect the envelopes. Apply PVA to both flaps, remove the scrap paper, place the cover on top, and press to adhere. Immediately remove the tape, open the covers, and firmly press the flaps and covers together to strengthen the join. Allow the glue to dry.

5. Apply PVA to the back of a remaining square of decorative paper and adhere it inside one front cover, covering the accordion flap. Trim the excess flush with the fore edge. (If making a gatefold, adhere 5 ¾″ x 6 ¼″ [13.3 x 15.8 cm] decorative-paper to the

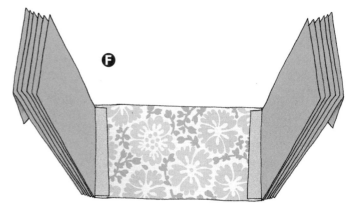

Glue accordions to back cover.

inside front covers.) Repeat with the other front cover.

6. Measure ⅝″ (1.6 cm) from the cover head and tail along the left edge, and mark. Apply double-stick tape to a ⅜″ (1 cm) -wide strip cut from a plastic file folder, and adhere it flush with the cover left edge. Mark eyelet holes ¼″ (6 mm) from the plastic-strip ends and punch ⅛″ (3 mm) holes through the plastic and cover. (If using a Japanese screw punch, place a small cutting mat underneath the cover

to prevent drilling through the book.) Insert and set the eyelets to hold the plastic strips. Repeat on the opposite front cover and the outside edges of the back cover.

Make the Closure

1. Punch a 1/8″ (3 mm) hole in the center of each plastic circle. Place a circle on each half of the front cover, and mark the cover through the holes. Punch 1/8″ (3 mm) holes in the covers at the marks. Insert an eyelet into one circle. Make a small loop with a slipknot at one end of the 16″ (40.6 cm) linen thread; slip the loop over the eyelet prong. Tighten the knot and trim the thread tail to 1/4″ (6 mm). Insert the eyelet into the cover, and then set it from the underside (**G**). Insert an eyelet into the other circle and set it on the other front cover. Tie the thread in a figure eight around the circles to fasten.

Make the File-Folder Calendars

1. Cut twelve 4 1/2″ x 7″ (11.4 x 17.8 cm) rectangles from file folders, incorporating the tabs, and measuring the length from the top of the tab. Fold the rectangles widthwise, leaving the tab showing, to create mini file folders. Stamp, or computer generate, small calendars on cardstock; cut out. Adhere a calendar to the front of each folder. Adhere the miniature folders to the envelopes. Working through the envelope front layer only, affix photo turns with miniature brads. The photo turns swivel to hold the files closed.

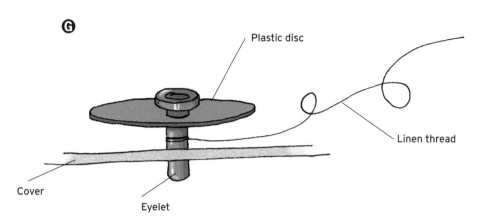

G

Plastic disc

Linen thread

Cover

Eyelet

Attach plastic circles to front covers.

TRY THIS

- This book allows for countless uses. It can hold greeting cards, bills and receipts, letters, business cards, tickets, or recipes. The length of the accordion binding can be varied to accommodate more or fewer envelopes.

- Instead of a gatefold, make a one-sided accordion book by cutting 9 1/2″ x 6 1/4″ (24.1 x 15.8 cm) covers and securing an accordion to only the left side.

- Vary the cover design by omitting the plastic strips and adding pieces of decorative paper, cardstock, or other embellishments.

Woven-Ticket Mini Book

BINDING STYLE: **SINGLE SIGNATURE SEWN TO WOVEN COVER** | APPROXIMATE FINISHED SIZE: 3″ x 5″ (7.6 x 12.7 cm)

A couple rolls of tickets from the office supply store can yield countless books at very little cost. The binding takes advantage of the book's woven structure, slipping back and forth between cover and signature. The books have a small profile, perfect for a pocket or briefcase, and can be put together quickly—ideal for making multiples.

TIP
Use graphics from old wall calendars or decorative file folders for the inside covers.

Materials

- 2″ x 1″ (5.1 x 2.5 cm) tickets: 6 strips of 4 each, one color, for covers
- 10 strips of 3 tickets each, in another color, for the covers
- nine 5 ¾″ x 5″ (14.6 x 12.7 cm) sheets text-weight paper for signature, grain short, folded in half widthwise (Set aside one folio for signature-punching template. Group remaining into one signature.)
- two 3″ x 5″ (7.6 x 12.7 cm) decorative-cardstock or paper rectangles for inside covers
- 8 ½″ x 11″ (21.6 x 27.9 cm) scrap paper
- repositionable low-tack tape
- glue stick
- 30″ (76.2 cm) of waxed linen thread
- bookbinding needle

Prepare the Covers

1. On the 8 ½″ x 11″ (21.6 x 27.9 cm) scrap paper, align three four-ticket strips right-side up and vertically so they butt up against each other and are even across the top. Measure 1 ½″ (3.8 cm) from the top, and then align the lower edge of low-tack tape across all three rows at the mark, securing the tickets to the paper. Secure the ticket lower edges to the paper with another piece of low-tack tape **(A)**.

2. Begin weaving the three-ticket strips horizontally just below the tape. Weave the first strip over the first vertical row, under the next, and then over the last row. Begin the second strip under the first vertical row. Continue this pattern until five strips are woven. Align and center the horizontal strips and butt them together, leaving no gaps **(B)**. Secure both ends of the horizontal strips to the paper with low-tack tape.

3. Turn the paper over and carefully peel it away from the tape, making sure the tape remains secured to the tickets. With the ticket wrong sides facing up, fold over the top, middle, and bottom overhanging tickets of the horizontal rows, aligning the folds with the edge of the vertical tickets. Secure the folded tickets to the back with a glue stick. **(C)**.

4. Fold in the overhanging tickets of the middle vertical row. Remove the tape and trim the remaining overhanging tickets flush with the cover **(D)**. Secure the loose flaps with a glue stick. The cover should measure approximately 3 ⅛″ x 5 ⅛″ (7.9 x 13 cm). Repeat the steps to weave the other cover. Attach the 3″ x 5″ (7.6 x 12.7 cm) decorative-cardstock rectangles to the cover wrong sides with the glue stick.

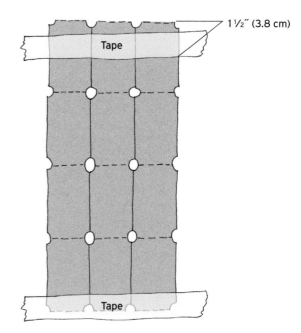

Ⓐ

1 ½″ (3.8 cm)

Tape

Tape

Tape tickets to paper.

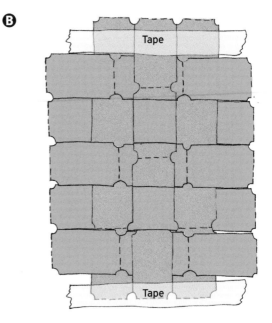

Ⓑ

Tape

Tape

Weave tickets through vertical rows.

C

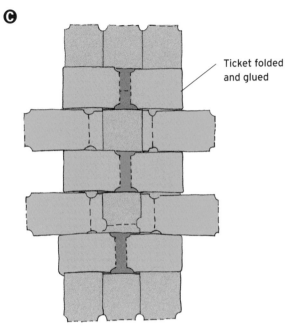

Ticket folded and glued

Fold in upper, middle, and botom rows.

D

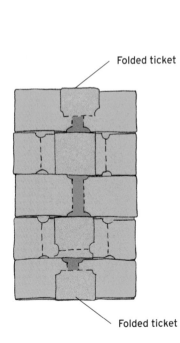

Folded ticket

Folded ticket

Fold in middle vertical row; trim remaining tickets.

Prepare the Signature

1. With one cover face up, center the folded paper for the signature-punching template on the cover with the fold about ⅛″ (3 mm) away from the spine edge. Make marks on the fold where the tickets abut, making four marks total **(E)**. Punch the signature using the template.

E

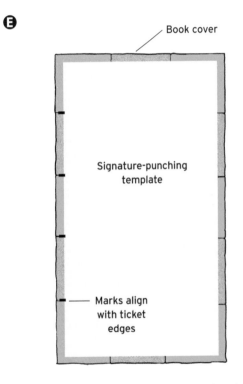

Book cover

Signature-punching template

Marks align with ticket edges

Use cover as guide to mark signature template.

Sew the Book

1. Thread the needle with waxed linen thread. Beginning on the front cover, slip the needle under the first horizontal ticket at the tail edge near the spine; leave a 6″ (15.2 cm) tail. Pick up the signature, and enter the bottom hole from the outside. Exit the next hole in the signature, and then pass the needle under the middle horizontal ticket at the spine. Snug the thread to the spine edge (figure shows the signature and spine separated to reveal the stitching, but they should be sewn close together). Go back into the signature at the corresponding hole; exit the next hole. Pass the needle under the top horizontal ticket, again snugging the thread to the spine **(F)**.

F

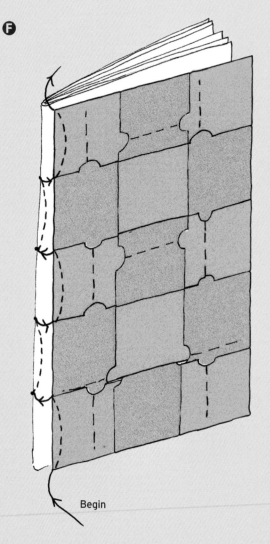

Begin

Stitch front cover to signature.

TRY THIS

- This structure has endless possibilities—it can be sewn with only two covers, or made into a multiple-signature accordion book by continuing to attach covers and signatures.
- Vary the ticket-strip lengths to make the book larger or smaller.
- Take advantage of blank tickets by stamping a design or monogram in the empty space.
- Use this design to make cards, invitations, or programs.
- Try a variety of ticket colors for vibrant covers.

G

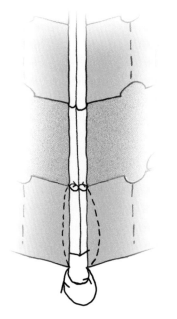

Pass thread under book, under lower ticket, and then into signature.

2. Pick up the back cover, bring the thread across the top of the signature, and then pass the needle under the top horizontal ticket. A small amount of thread will be visible at the top of the signature. Sew the signature to the back cover, working down the spine in the same manner.

3. Bring the thread underneath the book to the front, pass the needle under the horizontal ticket on the front cover, and then enter the signature at the bottom hole. Remove the needle and rethread it with the tail thread. Bring the tail thread underneath the book in the opposite direction, pass the needle under the horizontal ticket on the back cover, and enter the signature at the bottom hole **(G)**. Two small threads will be visible at the bottom. Open the book to the middle of the signature, and slip the needle under the lower binding stitches **(H)**. Tie the threads in a square knot and trim to ¼˝ (6 mm).

H

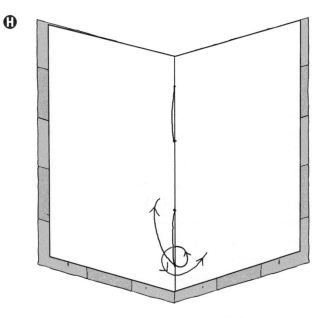

Pass thread under binding stitches.

CHAPTER 5

Dive In:
The Art of
Dumpster Diving

Amazing book-making ingredients can be found sifting through trash: furniture, fabric, packaging, clothing, toys, and appliances are just a few of the serviceable items that end up in dumpsters. Although dumpster diving has gained some mainstream respect, going through that trash still takes being intrepid and tenacious, and it's best to know what's in store before diving in.

Research local laws about dumpster diving. Many areas prohibit the activity or have restrictions due to property and privacy laws. Also, an etiquette code exists in the dumpster arena: don't take more than you need, and leave the area tidy.

This is a messy business, so dress appropriately: heavy gloves, long sleeves and pants, and sturdy shoes are a must. Tools of the trade include a long pole with a hook for fishing out items, strong trash bags or boxes to store your finds, and a stepladder to access the bin interior. Be sure to carry a flashlight. Dumpsters are often in alleyways, so it's a good idea to go with a friend, even during the day.

Safety is a paramount concern. Use extreme caution when handling trash or rummaging in bins. Hazards can include broken glass, medical waste, and animals. Watch for unsteady lids that can easily slam shut, and be on the lookout for trash trucks, which can pick up and dump a trash bin in seconds.

What you'll find will depend on where and when you look. However, the basic rules of usable bookbinding supplies apply: Look for relatively flat, sturdy items for covers, durable fibers for bindings, and smaller items to adorn your creations. And, be sure to clean salvaged items before bringing them into your home. While on the prowl you may encounter other divers, some of whom may be happy to trade information on good sites.

If the thought of poking through trash elicits a chill, there are other, less messy ways to find recyclable material. Freecycle groups on the Web are dedicated to giving away unwanted items within local communities. Craigslist.org, the popular online classified site, also has a category for free merchandise in different cities and states. Or start your own recycling program at work, at school, or in your neighborhood—encourage others to take part.

In this chapter, a game board becomes a travel journal, complete with a discarded jewelry box that holds pens, brushes, and watercolors. Two paint-by-number canvases are reborn as a guest book, and books destined for the landfill get a new life as a roll-up field journal.

- two 7 ⅜″ x 8 ½″ (18.8 x 21.6 cm) game-board rectangles for covers

- 3 ⅜″ x 9 ½″ (8.6 x 24.1 cm) suede, leather, or faux leather rectangle for cover

- 3 ⅜″ x 8 ⅜″ (8.6 x 21.3 cm) rectangle suede, leather, or faux leather rectangle for cover

- 300-grit sandpaper

- four 6 ¾″ (17.1 cm) strips cigar-box trim for covers (Peel from cigar box edges. Unused cigar box trim can be purchased online.)

- two 8 ½″ (12.6 cm) strips cigar-box trim for covers

- two 6 ¾″ x 8 ½″ (17.1 x 21.6 cm) cardstock rectangles for inside covers

- 40″ x 8 ¼″ (101.5 x 20.9 cm) cardstock rectangle for accordion, grain short

- seventeen 9 ½″ x 8 ¼″ (24.1 x 20.9 cm) sheets text-weight paper, grain short, folded in half (Reserve one folded page for signature-punching template; nest remaining into four signatures of four folios each.)

Game-Board Travel Journal

BINDING STYLE:
ACCORDION BINDING WITH PAMPHLET STITCHING
APPROXIMATE FINISHED SIZE:
7 ³/₈″ x 8 ½″ (18.8 x 21.6 cm)

Travelers tend to amass mountains of ephemera, from ticket stubs to maps, plus programs and packaging. What better way to preserve your adventures than in a book filled with pockets and pages? The accordion binding in this journal can be flipped page by page, or pulled out for a panoramic view. The covers come from a board game, the spine is from an old suede jacket, and the closure is made from a man's tie. The added bonus is a detachable box that holds pens, pencils, paint, and paintbrushes for when the artistic mood strikes. The accordion pages are customizable—add or subtract pockets, sew in additional pages, and move elements around. It's the perfect traveling companion.

- 6 ¾″ x 5 ½″ (17.1 x 14 cm) cardstock rectangle, cut and scored with gusseted-pocket template (page 132)
- 4 ¾″ x 2 ½″ (12.1 x 6.4 cm) cardstock rectangle for gusseted-pocket flap
- 1″ x 3 ½″ (2.5 x 8.9 cm) cardstock for gusseted-pocket tab
- 2″ x ½″ (5.1 x 1.3 cm) cardstock for gusseted-pocket closure
- 4 ⅞″ x 8 ¼″ (12.4 x 22.2 cm) cardstock rectangle, cut with slash-pocket template (page 133)
- 5 ½″ x 5 ¼″ (14 x 14.6 cm) cardstock rectangle, cut and scored with angled-pocket template (page 134)
- two 9 ½″ x 2 ¼″ (24.1 x 2.7 cm) cardstock strips, grain short, for pamphlet-stitched panels
- 9 ½″ x 3 ½″ (24.1 x 8.9 cm) cardstock strip, grain short, for pamphlet-stitched panels
- 8 ½″ x 11″ (21.6 x 27.9 cm) decorative paper or map rectangle for envelope (Cut, score, and mark sewing holes with envelope template.) (page 133)
- two ¾″ (1.9 cm) -diameter cardstock circles
- two ⅛″ (3 mm) eyelets, eyelet setting tools
- 2 ⅛″ x 8 ⅛″ x 1″ (5.4 x 20.6 x 2.5 cm) cardboard jewelry box, or box with similar dimensions
- maps for covering jewelry box
- soft matte gel medium
- foam brush
- 8 ¼″ (20.9 cm) of ⅝″ (1.6 cm) -wide grosgrain ribbon
- 20 ½″ (52.1 cm) of ⅝″ (1.6 cm) -wide grosgrain ribbon
- two ½″ (1.3 cm) strips of ⅝″ (1.6 cm) -wide hook-and-loop tape
- man's tie
- two rivets, rivet setting tools
- sewing machine, needle, and thread
- ⅛″ (3 mm) -hole punch
- waxed linen thread and bookbinding needle
- PVA, glue stick, and strong double-stick tape
- straight pins
- angled-pocket template (page 134)
- envelope pattern (page 133)
- gusseted-pocket template (page 132)
- slash-pocket template (page 133)

Prepare the Covers

1. Apply PVA to the back of one 6 ¾″ (17.1 cm) strip of cigar-box trim and adhere it to the front cover upper edge, encasing the edge so the trim shows equally on the inside and outside. Adhere another 6 ¾″ (17.1 cm) strip to the front cover lower edge. Adhere an 8 ½″ (12.6 cm) strip along the fore edge. Repeat for the back cover.

2. Measure 1″ (2.5 cm) from the front and back cover spine edges and draw a light pencil line. Lightly sand both covers up to the lines; this will help the glue adhere. Apply PVA to the front cover up to the line. Adhere the 3 ⅜″ x 9 ½″ (8.6 x 24.1 cm) suede strip to the cover, aligning the suede's long edge with the line, and leaving ½″ (1.3 cm) overhanging at the head and tail edges. Turn the cover over, measure 1 ⅜″ (3.5 cm) from the spine edge onto the suede, and draw a pencil or pen line. Apply PVA to the right of the line **(A)**. Adhere the suede to the back cover, making sure the front and back covers are aligned horizontally.

3. If the inside covers are slick, sand lightly to allow the suede to adhere better. Apply glue to the overhanging suede edges and fold them to the inside, making sure the suede adheres to itself in the spine.

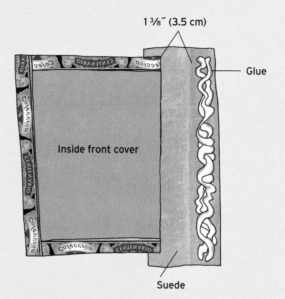

1 ⅜″ (3.5 cm)

Glue

Suede

Glue suede to covers with space between spine edges.

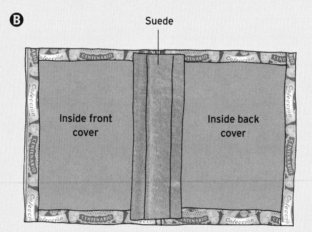

Suede

Apply glue to the remaining suede strip and adhere it inside the cover, overlapping the spine **(B)**. With a bone folder, gently smooth the suede against the inside edges of the cover boards to ensure contact.

Make the Accordion

1. Make marks 5″ (12.7 cm) apart on the long edges of the 40″ (101.5 cm) cardstock strip. Align a ruler with the marks and score across the cardstock. Fan-fold the card-stock, making sure the folds are aligned and resulting in eight 5″ (12.7 cm) -wide panels. (If a 40″ [101.5 cm] length of cardstock is unavailable, glue folded pieces together– see "Twelve-Month Organizer, Make the Accordion Bindings" on page 65.)

2. The following through step 6 are attached to the accordion panels as it unfolds to the left. When placing a pocket into a valley fold, leave at least a ⅛″ (3 mm) gap just before the fold to allow the book to close.

3. Construct the gusseted pocket. Accordion-fold the pocket side edges, and then fold up the lower edge. Fold under one long edge of the flap ½″ (1.3 cm). Attach the ½″ (1.3 cm) fold to the back of the pocket where it hits the side accordion folds. Adhere the tab to the center point of the flap front edge. (Round off the flap and tab corners if desired.) Sew the closure-strip ends to the pocket front with a cross-stitch and waxed linen thread; the tab should slip easily into the closure. Apply double-stick tape to the pocket and flap folded edges on the back, and adhere

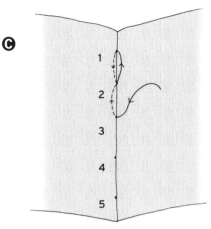

C

Begin stitching through center point.

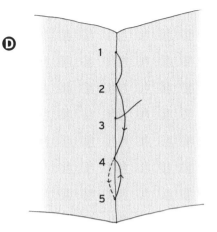

D

Take long stitch to lower holes and sew.

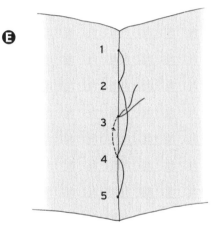

E

Go back to center hole and tie off thread.

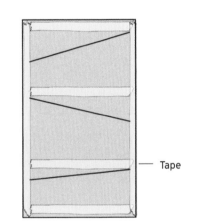

F

Tape

Apply tape to slash pocket back.

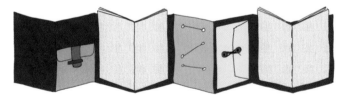

Accordian pages as they're pulled to the left

Accordian pages as they're pulled to the right

the pocket to the second accordion panel.

4. Mark the extra folio page on the fold to make the signature-punching template. Mark ½″ and 2 ¼″ (1.3 cm and 5.7 cm) from the head and tail edges, and then mark the fold midpoint. Place a text-page signature between the accordion third and fourth panels, and then use the template to punch holes in the signature and accordion with an awl. Attach the signature with a five-hole pamphlet stitch. Thread the bookbinding needle with 30″ (76.2 cm) of waxed linen thread and enter hole #3 from the inside; leave a 3″ (7.6 cm) tail. Enter hole #2 from the outside, enter hole #1 from the inside, go back through hole #2 from the outside **(C)**. Enter hole #4 from the inside, enter hole #5 from the outside, and go back through hole #4 from the inside **(D)**. Enter hole #3 from the outside, and come out on one side of the center stitch, opposite the tail thread **(E)**. Tie the ends in a square knot and trim to ¼″ (6 mm). Repeat to sew another text-page signature between the seventh and eighth panels.

5. Apply double-stick tape to the back of the slash pocket and adhere it to the fifth panel **(F)**.

6. Center the envelope on the fold between the fifth and sixth panels with the

envelope right side facing the accordion. Punch the designated holes through the envelope and the accordion. Sew a pamphlet stitch with 16″ (40.6 cm) of waxed linen thread to secure the envelope (see step 8). Fold up and glue the envelope sides. Punch a ⅛″ (3 mm) hole in the center of both cardstock circles, place one close to the lower edge of the envelope flap, and one about ½″ (1.3 cm) below on the envelope body. Mark through the circle centers and punch only the envelope top layer with a ⅛″ (3 mm) hole punch. Push an eyelet through one circle. Tie a loose slipknot at the end of a 12″ (30.5 cm) length of waxed linen thread, slip the loop around the eyelet prong, and then tighten the knot; trim the tail to ¼″ (6 mm). Push the eyelet through the envelope flap and set it with the eyelet-setting tools (see "Twelve-Month Organizer, Make the Closure" on page 67). Push the other eyelet through the remaining circle, through the envelope, and set the eyelet. Tie the thread in a figure eight around the circles to close the envelope.

7. The following through step 9 are added to the accordion as it unfolds to the right. Stitch a text-page signature between the second and third panel using the five-hole pamphlet stitch (see step 4). Repeat to sew a signature between the sixth and seventh panels.

8. Fold the 2 ¼″ and 3 ½″ (2.7 cm and 8.9 cm) -wide cardstock panels in half widthwise. Make three marks in the fold of each: one at the fold midpoint, and two ¼″ (6 mm) from either edge. Align the cardstock folds with the accordion fold between the fourth and fifth panels. Place the two narrower panels flush with the head and tail edges, center the wider panel between the two, and leave a ⅛″ (3 mm) gap between each of them. Punch holes through the panels and accordion at the marks. For each, thread the bookbinding needle with 12″ (30.5 cm) of waxed linen thread. Enter the middle hole from the inside, leaving a 2″ (5.1 cm) tail. Enter the top hole from the outside and enter the bottom hole from the inside (G). Enter the middle hole from the outside, making sure not to split the threads, and come up on the opposite side of the center stitch than the tail thread (H). Tie the ends in a square knot and trim to ¼″ (6 mm). Repeat to stitch the other two panels.

9. Fold in the sides and lower edge of the angled pocket, and then apply double-stick tape to the flaps. Adhere the pocket to the sixth panel of the accordion.

G

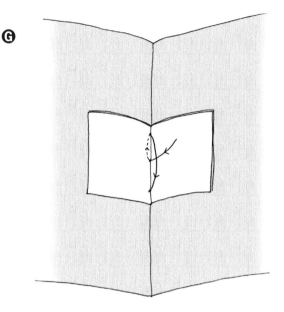

Begin through inside center hole.

H

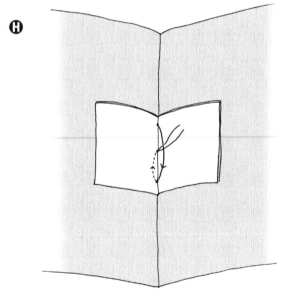

Come out at center and tie knot.

Make the Box

1. Tear the maps into small strips. With a foam brush, apply a thin layer of soft-matte gel medium to the back of the strips and adhere them to the inside and outside of the box and lid until they are covered; let dry. (Don't layer too much paper around the box edges or it won't close.) Seal with a thin layer of gel medium; let dry.

2. Position the box on one 6 ¾˝ x 8 ½˝ (17.1 x 21.6 cm) cardstock rectangle a scant ⅛˝ (3 mm) from the right edge, and centering it between the head and tail edges; trace around the box. Remove the box, and center both pieces of grosgrain ribbon across the drawn rectangle. Mark the ribbon widths where they intersect the box tracing. Cut slits between the marks with a craft knife (I), and then erase the pencil marks.

3. Fold under one end of the longer ribbon ½˝ (1.3 cm) and secure with a glue stick. Machine or hand-sew the hook section of the hook-and-loop tape to the folded end, covering the ribbon's raw end. With the hook section facing up, thread the ribbon's opposite end through the lower rectangle slit and out the top slit. Fold under the other end ½˝ (1.3 cm), secure with glue, and then sew the loop section of the tape so it faces down and covers the ribbon's

raw end (J). Place the box on the cardstock, and wrap the ribbon around the box, adjusting the ribbon so the closure is at the box lower edge. Undo the ribbon, remove the box, turn the cardstock over, and secure the ribbon with a glue stick. Repeat for the 8 ¼˝ (20.9 cm) ribbon, making sure the closure is on the right edge of the box.

Assemble the Book

1. Apply PVA to the back of the cardstock with the ribbons, and adhere it to the inside back cover, flush with the fore edge, head, and tail (the cardstock will overlap the suede). Apply PVA to the remaining piece of cardstock and glue it to the inside front cover. Allow the glue to dry. If the covers warp, press them under a heavy weight.

2. Open the accordion to the left, so the last panel is a valley fold. Slip a piece of scrap paper under the last accordion panel and apply PVA. Remove the scrap paper and adhere the panel to the inside back cover, flush with the spine edge. There should be a ¼˝ (6 mm) space between the folded accordion and the box. Make sure the accordion panel is completely adhered to the back cover.

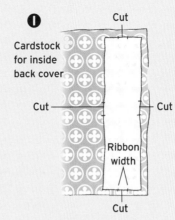

Mark ribbon locations on drawn rectangle.

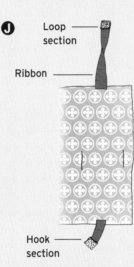

Fold in cut end corners and stitch together.

Make the Closure

1. Measure the tie 42˝ (1.1 m) from the narrow end and cut it straight across. Remove about 1˝ (2.5 cm) of the interfacing from the cut end. Fold the end ¼˝ (6 mm) to the inside; press. Turn in the corners to form a triangle, and stitch closed (K). The seam on the back of the tie is often loosely stitched; reinforce the seam with hemstitching.

2. With a hand or rotary drill, or a Japanese screw punch fitted with a 2.5-mm or 3-mm tip, punch a ⅛˝ (3 mm) hole in the front cover, ½˝ (1.3 cm) to the right of the suede, and centered between the head and tail edges. Insert the male part of the rivet from inside the cover. Find the midpoint of the tie and mark with a pin. Align the pin with the spine, and place the tie over the rivet; mark the rivet position on the tie with a pen. Punch a ⅛˝ (3 mm) hole through the tie, and then push the hole onto the rivet. Place the female rivet part on top and set the rivet according to the manufacturer's instructions. Repeat for the back cover. Remove the pin. Fasten the tie ends into a square knot.

Paint-by-Number Guest Book

BINDING STYLE: STAB BINDING | APPROXIMATE FINISHED SIZE: 11 ¾" x 10 ½" (29.8 x 26.7 cm)

Paint-by-number canvases have tremendous kitsch value, so discovering one in a trash bin is a true find. Made into books, they transform into works of art, worthy of being front and center as a guest book for a party. This structure is easily put together with duct tape, suede lacing, and an old paintbrush. This larger size is also perfect for a drawing or writing journal, but canvases come in all sizes and can be cut to any dimensions.

Materials

- three paint-by-number canvases: one 11 ¾" x 10 ½" (29.8 x 26.7 cm) rectangle for the back, one 10" x 10 ½" (25.4 x 26.7 cm) rectangle for the cover, and one 1 ¾" x 10 ½" (4.4 x 26.7 cm) strip for the cover hinge (Pieces can be cut from larger canvases.)

- 11 ¾" x 10 ½" (29.8 x 26.7 cm) decorative-cardstock rectangle for inside back cover

- 10" x 10 ½" (25.4 x 26.7 cm) decorative-cardstock rectangle for inside front cover

- 1 ½" x 10 ½" (3.8 x 26.7 cm) strip decorative cardstock for inside hinge

- sixteen 11 ½" x 10 ½" (29.2 x 26.7 cm) sheets cardstock or drawing paper for inside pages, grain short

- duct tape

- acrylic spray sealer

- paintbrush, approximately 7" to 8" (17.8 cm to 20.3 cm) long

- 14" (35.6 cm) of ⅛" (3 mm) -wide suede lacing

- hand or electric drill, or Japanese screw punch

- binder clips

- PVA

- thick craft glue

Prepare the Covers

1. Spray the covers and hinge piece with two or three coats of acrylic sealer; let dry between each coat. Glue the cardstock rectangles to the canvas wrong sides with PVA. If canvases warp after gluing, press them under a heavy weight.

2. Tear a strip of 11 ½″ (29.2 cm) duct tape, and then cut two ¾″ (1.9 cm) -wide strips from it (see Tip on opposite page for cutting duct tape). Use one strip to attach the cover hinge to the front cover, leaving a ¼″ (6 mm) gap between the pieces, and overlapping the canvases ¼″ (6 mm) **(A)**. Trim the tape flush with the head and tail edges. Turn the cover over and tape the underside, making sure the tape pieces adhere to each other in the gap.

3. Wrap the canvas edges with duct tape. Tear pieces about 1″ (2.5 cm) longer than each side and trim the tape to ½″ (1.3 cm) wide. Apply the tape to the head and tail edges first, overlapping the edge ¼″ (6 mm) and leaving a ½″ (1.3 cm) overhang at each end. Fold the tape over the edge, so ¼″ (6 mm) of tape overlaps the inside edge. Trim the ends flush with the cover. Repeat to add tape to the remaining edges.

A

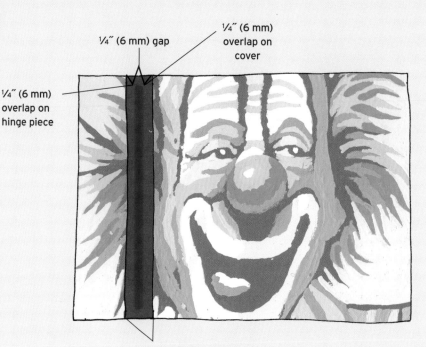

¼″ (6 mm) gap

¼″ (6 mm) overlap on cover

¼″ (6 mm) overlap on hinge piece

¾″ (1.9 cm) -wide tape

Tape front cover to hinge.

TRY THIS

Paint-by-number canvases also make great journal covers bound with other types of stab bindings; instructions are available on the Internet and in bookbinding books.

Bind the Book

1. Score each 11 ½" x 10 ½" (29.2 x 26.7 cm) sheet of cardstock 1 ⁷⁄₈" (4.7 cm) from the left edge **(B)**.

2. Center the paintbrush on the cover hinge and mark two holes directly underneath the handle, about 4" (10.2 cm) apart **(C)**. Place the stacked text pages between the covers, flush with the left edge of the book. Clamp the book together with binder clips, and drill two ³⁄₁₆" (4.8 mm) holes. (If using a Japanese screw punch, fit it with the 4-mm tip and punch the covers and pages separately.) If the pages expand after drilling, pinch them back together.

3. Set the paintbrush on the hinge, and secure it with a bit of craft glue. Begin at the lower hole, and thread the 14" (35.6 cm) suede lace through the hole from the back, leaving a 3" (7.6 cm) tail. Wrap the lace around the paintbrush handle and go back through the same hole. Keeping the lace taut, bring it up through the top hole, wrap it around the paintbrush, and go back through the hole **(D)**. Bring the lace back down to the bottom hole, and tie the ends in a square knot.

B

1 ⁷⁄₈" (4.7 cm)

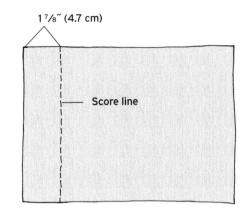

Score line

Score the cardstock pages.

C

Hole

Mark the hole locations.

D

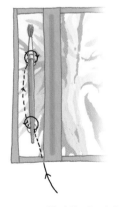

Bind the book together.

> **TIP**
>
> To cut duct tape, tear a piece from the roll and press it lightly onto wax paper. Mark the desired width using a pencil, and cut the tape with a craft knife and metal ruler backed with sandpaper. The sandpaper prevents the ruler from sliding on the slippery tape. The tape is still sticky after being stuck to the wax paper.

Roll-Up Field Journal

BINDING STYLE: **SEWN-THROUGH-THE-SPINE BINDING** | APPROXIMATE FINISHED SIZE: 8 ½″ x 9 ½″ (21.6 x 24.1 cm)

Books are treasures, but unfortunately many volumes end up in landfills. Before they reach their final resting place, salvage them, and remake them into field journals. This project rescues the cover spines from discarded hardback books, rolls up neatly to fit into a tote bag or backpack, and unfurls to become a handy tracker of flora and fauna. The rigid spine to which the signatures are sewn is courtesy of an old ruler. The book's lining is cut from a man's shirt, and artificial leaves decorate the cover and interior—trash most certainly turned into treasure.

Materials

- 11 to 13 hardback books with bookcloth spines, approximately 9 ½″ (24.1 cm) tall
- 26 ½″ x 10 ½″ (67.3 x 26.7 cm) rectangle cut from the back of a man's extra-large cotton shirt (or use lightweight cotton fabric)
- seventeen 18″ x 8″ (45.7 x 20.3 cm) rectangles of lightweight, flexible drawing paper, such as Ingres (Fold pages in half widthwise. Reserve one folio for signature-punching template. Nest remaining into four signatures of four folios each.)
- 8 ½″ (21.6 cm) section from ruler or yardstick, 1″ to 1 ¼″ (2.5 x 3.1 cm) wide
- 100-grit sandpaper
- two 30″ (76.2 cm) lengths waxed linen thread
- 25 ½″ x 9 ½″ (64.8 x 24.1 cm) rectangle of double-sided fusible web for cover, plus extra to adhere leaves if desired
- large two-part grommet for closure, grommet-setting tools
- 23″ of ¼″ (59 cm) -wide strip of sturdy leather
- several faux leaves for embellishment
- thick craft glue
- repositionable low-tack tape
- hand or electric drill
- bookbinding needle
- rotary cutter and quilt ruler (optional)
- sewing machine or needle and thread
- small saw
- spine punching template (page 139)

Prepare the Cover

1. Separate the pages from the found books by holding the covers open and firmly pulling the text block. The pages will start to pull away at the hinges where the text block is connected to the front and back covers. Begin cutting at the top of the front hinge with a craft knife, working carefully down the book without cutting into the spine. Repeat on the back until the entire text block is removed.

2. Remove the bookcloth by peeling it away from the spine head and tail edges inside the covers **(A)**. If it doesn't peel easily, lift it off with a craft knife that has a dull blade. Work slowly, and peel the bookcloth from the covers, salvaging as much as possible. Once removed, the bookcloth will probably have paper glued to the back. Peel off what you can, and then use the 100-grit sandpaper to remove the rest. Take care when sanding so you don't create holes. Some paper residue can remain as long as the spine is flexible. Trim the spine long edges to make them straight, but leave the head and tail edges intact. Repeat to prepare all the spines. Place the spines side by side, overlapping the edges about ¼" to ½" (6 mm to 1.3 cm), until the total width is 26" (66 cm).

3. Overlap the spines about ¼" to ½" (6 mm to 1.3 cm), and sew them together by hand or machine. Incorporate the leaves by slipping them between the spines and catching them in the stitching **(B)**. Trim any loose threads. Cut the sewn spines into a 24 ½" x 8 ½" (62.2 x 21.6 cm) rectangle—a rotary cutter and quilt ruler work well for this. Tack down the loose edges of the leaves with a sewing machine, with needle and thread, or with double-sided fusible web, resulting in a pliable pieced fabric.

4. Center and fuse the 25 ½" x 9 ½" (64.8 x 24.1 cm) double-sided fusible web to the wrong side of the fabric rectangle following the manufacturer's instructions. Remove the paper backing, and then center the pieced spines faceup over the web side of the fabric; trim the fabric flush with the spines. Fuse the fabric and spines together. Trim away any overhanging fabric, and then stitch the perimeter of the fused rectangle. Add more leaves to both sides of the cover with fusible web if desired.

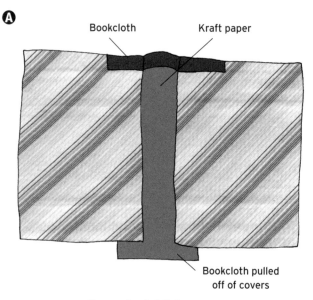

A

Bookcloth   Kraft paper

Bookcloth pulled off of covers

Remove bookcloth from covers.

B

Sew spines together.

Prepare the Signatures

1. Mark the reserved folio along the fold ½" (1.3 cm) from the upper and lower edges and at the midpoint; use as the template to punch holes in the four signatures.

Sew the Book

1. Measure 9 ½″ (24.1 cm) from the right edge of the cover, and mark the head and tail edges for the spine location. Lightly sand the back of the ruler to remove any varnish. Apply a layer of thick craft glue to the back of the ruler and adhere it to the cover with the right edge of the ruler aligned with the marks. Allow the glue to dry.

2. Copy and adhere the spine-punching template on page 139 to the top of the ruler with repositionable low-tack tape. (The template is for a 1 ⅛″ (2.8 cm) -wide ruler; if your ruler width is slightly different, center the template on the ruler.) With a hand or an electric drill, drill the holes where noted. Make sure the drill bit creates a hole large enough to accommodate a needle threaded with waxed linen thread.

Begin at lower edge and work towards top.

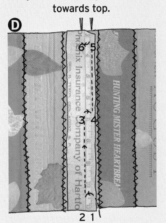

Work down spine to complete stitching.

Attach leather strip through grommet.

3. Signatures are sewn directly to the spine through the ruler. Thread the binding needle with 30″ of waxed linen thread. Enter hole #1 of the first signature from the inside, leaving a 3″ (7.6 cm) tail. Secure the tail inside the signature with low-tack repositionable tape, and keep the thread taut as you sew the binding. Enter hole #2 from the outside, and pick up the second signature. Enter hole #3 from the inside, and then enter hole #4 from the outside, going back into the first signature. Enter hole #5 from the inside, and then enter hole #6 from the outside, going back into the second signature (C). Enter hole #3 from the inside. Enter hole #4 from the outside, going back into the first signature, and being careful not to split the threads (D). Tie off the threads with a square knot at hole #1 inside the first signature; trim the ends to ¼″ (6 mm). Repeat to sew the remaining two signatures.

Make the Closure

1. Find the midpoint of the back cover, and set the two-part grommet ½″ (1.3 cm) from the edge, following the manufacturer's instructions. Punch a ³⁄₁₆″ (4.8 mm) hole, or cut a small slit about ½″ (1.3 cm) from one leather-strip end, parallel to the long edges. Taper the opposite end. With the cover facing up, feed the tapered end of the leather strip up through the grommet, and then thread the tapered end through the hole (E). Roll up the book, and wrap the leather around it to hold it closed.

TRY THIS

- Instead of cutting paper to size for the text block, tear it for a deckled edge. Hold a metal-edge ruler firmly over the paper, and tear the paper against the ruler.
- Can't find enough book spines? Intersperse them with strips of plain or patterned ready-made bookcloth or heavy fabric.
- Add faux flowers in addition to, or instead of, the leaves.

TIPS

- Not all hardback books have bookcloth spines; some are made of paper. Remove the book's paper jacket and rub your fingers along the spine. It should look and feel like cloth.
- Don't throw away unused book parts. Use the covers for handmade books, or cut and decorate them for drink coasters (finish with an acrylic spray sealer to make them water resistant). The inside pages are perfect for collage projects, cards, and text pages.

The Best Things in Bookbinding Are Free

Few things trump getting bookbinding supplies at zero cost. A keen eye, some ingenuity, and a little gentle persuasion are all it takes to come up with terrific materials that don't require a cent.

Consider gift cards—once the balance reaches zero, turn the small plastic rectangles into pocket-size books good for jotting notes. Or create mini journals from heavyweight glossy postcards, flyers, or brochures.

When freebies require a solicitation, politeness is always the rule of the game. Ask nicely for a couple of extra coasters from the bartender or waitress and he or she will likely oblige. Square coasters can be used to make up quick books in a number of binding styles, such as accordion and chain stitch. Sign shops usually have misprints of signage and vinyl banners, which typically get thrown out. Stop by and see whether some are available; pliable banners are great for sew-through-the-spine journals. Snag an extra pizza box or two and cut the cardboard tops into book and album covers.

Some carpet samples are hefty enough to house thick text blocks. More flexible carpets lend themselves to long-stitch bindings, while stiffer ones are better suited to open-spine styles. Outdated sewing-pattern books make chic covers, and the pages work as text pages or embellishments.

When and whom to ask is key in bagging free items. Pick a time when business isn't hectic and the staff is more relaxed. Going directly to the manager can often expedite the request. Don't be greedy—take only what you need.

It's likely you'll be asked what the items are for. Be honest—divulging the details of your project can pique interest, especially if you encounter a fellow artist. Whenever possible, thank those who have been generous by giving them a handmade book.

Books in this chapter include a mini note jotter made from gift cards with an attractive French-stitch binding. Coasters are fashioned into a piano-hinge cocktail-recipe book, with cocktail stirrers holding everything together. Pattern books are fashioned into a stylish purse-shaped journal sure to turn heads.

Pocket Gift-Card Book

BINDING STYLE: **FRENCH STITCH OVER TAPES** | APPROXIMATE FINISHED SIZE: 3 ³/₈″ x 2 ¹/₈″ (8.6 x 5.4 cm)

Gift cards don't have to be tossed when you've spent their value. Their sturdiness and durability make them perfect for books, and many are illustrated with attractive graphics. The petite size fits easily into a purse or pocket. The French-stitch binding allows the book to be opened flat, and it is both decorative and functional. Thread, ribbon, and eyelet colors enhance the overall design.

Materials

- two 3 ³/₈″ x 2 ¹/₈″ (8.6 x 5.4 cm) plastic gift cards

- thirty-seven 6 ½″ x 2″ (15.2 x 5.1 cm) sheets text-weight paper, grain short, folded in half widthwise (Set aside one folio for the signature-punching template. Group remaining into nine signatures of four folios each. Round the fore edge corners if desired.)

- 42″ (1.1 m) piece of waxed linen thread

- two 3 ³/₈″ x 2 ¹/₈″ (8.6 x 5.4 cm) sheets cardstock for the inside covers, corners rounded (A corner-rounder punch found in scrapbook aisle makes this easy.)

- two 4 ½″ (11.4 cm) lengths of ³/₈″ (1 cm) -wide gros-grain ribbon

- four ¹/₈″ (3 mm) eyelets and eyelet-setting tools

- low-tack tape or binder clips

- bookbinding needle

- screw punch

- seam sealant

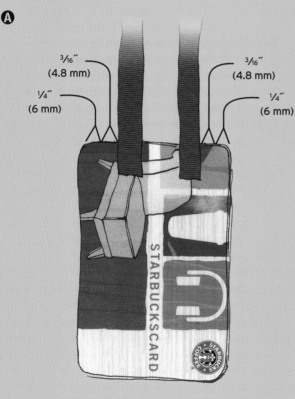

A

³/₁₆″ (4.8 mm)

³/₁₆″ (4.8 mm)

¼″ (6 mm)

¼″ (6 mm)

STARBUCKSCARD

Make signature-punching template.

Sewing the Text Block

1. Mark the signature-punching template on the fold ¼″ (6 mm) from either edge. Make another mark ³/₁₆″ (4.8 mm) away from each ¼″ (6 mm) mark. Place a ribbon just to the side of the ³/₁₆″ (4.8 mm) mark, and make another mark next to the ribbon's opposite edge. Do the same next to the other ³/₁₆″ (4.8 mm) mark **(A)**. Use the template to punch holes in the signatures with an awl.

2. Sew the signatures with the spine edge facing you. Stack signatures on top of each other as the book is sewn. Thread the needle with the waxed linen thread and pick up the first signature. Enter the first hole from the outside, leaving a 6˝ (15.2 cm) tail. Exit from the inside at the next hole. Place a ribbon across the spine, letting one ribbon end hang down 2˝ (5.1 cm) from the signature edge. Enter the next hole from the outside, capturing the ribbon as you pull the thread through. Enter the next hole from the inside and place the second ribbon across the signature, also with 2˝ (5.1 cm) hanging down. Enter the next hole from the outside, capturing the ribbon. Enter the next hole from the inside and exit. Pull the threads parallel to the spine to tighten. The ribbons should lie flat without bunching up. Close the first signature, and then place the next signature on top. Cross over into the second signature, entering the hole from the outside. Exit at the next hole, and slide the needle under the stitch that overlaps the ribbon directly below. Then enter the next hole in the second signature, linking the threads and capturing the ribbon. Exit at the next hole, repeat the linking stitch, go back inside the signature, and exit at the last hole **(B)**. Tighten the threads and tie a square knot; do not trim the thread. Close the signature.

3. Pick up the third signature, place it on top, cross over and enter the adjoining hole, and then exit the hole next to the ribbon. Slide the needle under the thread of the second signature that crosses the ribbon. Enter the next hole in the third signature, and exit next to the other ribbon, repeat the linking stitch, enter the hole on the opposite side of the ribbon, and exit the last hole. At the end of the signature, with the thread on the outside, do a kettle stitch—a small knot that helps stabilize the signatures. Slide the needle under the stitch that connects the two previous signatures, pulling the needle away from the text block. As the thread is pulled, a loop will form. Pass the needle through the loop and pull straight up, tightening the knot **(C)**.

4. Continue the sewing pattern until all signatures have been sewn. Do a double kettle stitch at the end of the last signature. Trim the thread ends, or pull them back into the first and last signature through the entry hole. Slip the needle under the nearest stitch inside the signature, form a loop, and bring the needle through the loop, making a knot **(D)**. Repeat, and trim ends to ¼˝ (6 mm).

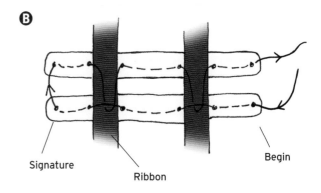

Stitch signatures, capturing the ribbons.

Signature

Ribbon

Begin

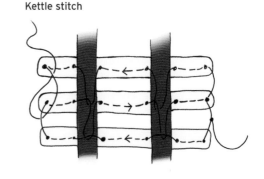

Kettle stitch

Join next signature, ending with kettle stitch.

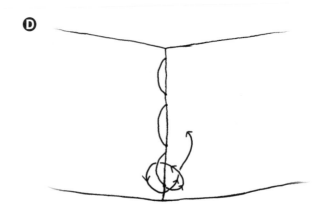

Tie knot inside signature.

Attach the Covers to the Text Block

1. To mark the placement for the eyelet holes, place the front cover over the text block, and pull the ribbons straight across the cover. Mark the holes 3/4″ (1.9 cm) from the spine, and centered underneath the ribbons. Stack the front and back covers as they will be when the book is bound, and secure them together with tape or binder clips. Punch or drill 1/8″ (3 mm) holes at the marks through both covers at the same time. Place the front cover on the text block, and mark corresponding holes on the ribbons; punch holes at the marks **(E)**. Set eyelets from the outside through the ribbon and cover, following the manufacturer's instructions. Attach the back cover the same way; trim the ribbon ends. If ribbons unravel, apply a seam sealant to the ends.

2. Cut the first and last pages of the text block in half and glue the remaining portion to the inside of the covers **(F)**. Glue the pieces of cardstock inside the covers, covering the half pages.

E

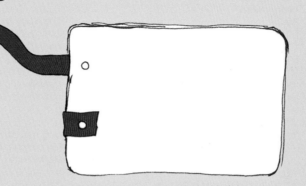

Punch holes in cover, and then punch ribbons.

F

First page glued to cover

Inside cover

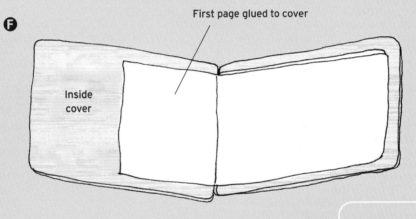

Cut pages and glue to cover.

TIPS

- When sewing the text block, open the signature being sewn and place a small weight in the middle. This keeps the signatures stable while sewing.
- Lay the signatures on a table, or a stack of books, with the spine extending past the edge to make sewing easier.

TRY THIS

- Orient the book vertically, using three ribbons across the spine instead of two and punching the appropriate amount of holes in the signatures to accommodate the extra ribbon. Always be sure to punch one hole at the head and tail for the kettle stitch.
- Use playing cards for covers; glue two or three together for added strength.

Coaster Cocktail-Recipe Book

BINDING STYLE: **PIANO-HINGE BINDING** | APPROXIMATE FINISHED SIZE: 4˝ (10.2 cm) square

Cocktail coasters may be considered throwaway items, but hold on to them when there's a book to be made. This handy cocktail-recipe book uses coasters as covers and pages, employs drink stirrers as hinges, and has an appetizer pick for the closure. The piano-hinge binding goes together easily and requires no sewing. Bar-coaster graphics are becoming more sophisticated, so it shouldn't be difficult finding ones that are eye-catching. This book makes a great shower, host, or housewarming gift, filled with instructions for making delicious libations.

Materials

- 5 bar coasters about 4˝ (10.2 cm) square, for covers and pages (Coasters may vary in size from 3 ¾˝ to 4 ¼˝ [9.5 cm to 10.8 cm].)
- 5 cocktail stirrers about 6˝ to 7˝ (15.2 cm to 17.8 cm) long
- sword-shaped appetizer pick
- 30˝ (76.2 cm) of ⅝˝ (1.6 cm) -wide twill tape or sturdy ribbon, cut into twenty 1 ½˝ (3.8 cm) pieces
- 42˝ (1.1 m) of ⅛˝ (3 mm) -wide double-face satin ribbon for binding and closure
- 3 ½˝ x 7˝ (8.9 x 17.8 cm) cardstock rectangles, folded in half widthwise, for recipes (size may vary, depending on coaster size)
- 3 ½˝ (8.9 cm) cardstock squares for recipes (sizes may vary)
- eighteen ⅛˝ (3 mm) eyelets, eyelet-setting tools
- ⅛˝ (3 mm) hole punch or Japanese screw punch fitted with 2.5-mm or 3-mm tip
- glue stick
- super glue
- piano-hinge template (page 135)

Prepare the Piano-Hinge Binding

1. Transfer the marks from the piano-hinge template on page 135 to the left side of four coasters. For the fifth coaster, mark just the first and third ⅝˝ (1.6 cm) spaces from the top using the template. (This template will work for different size coasters and ensures the hinge-tab alignment. Align the template midpoint with the midpoint of the coaster's side.) Every ⅝˝ (1.6 cm) -wide space is where the twill tape is glued. On each coaster, draw a light pencil line ¼˝ (6 mm) from the left edge. Draw a ¼˝ (6 mm) line from the same edge on the coaster back.

TIPS
- Spray the coasters with acrylic sealer to make them less porous—the sealer may slightly discolor the coasters; test first.
- If a stirrer won't fit through the tabs, wrap the tabs around the stirrer, glue the tabs in place, and then set the eyelets.

TRY THIS
Use coasters as front and back covers, and attach tabs to cardstock for the inside pages.

2. Create a binding tab by applying glue stick to ¼″ (6 mm) of the end of a twill tape piece. Place the twill tape on the front of the coaster, between the first two marks, and align the end with the ¼″ (6 mm) line. Repeat to attach three more twill pieces. Apply glue to ¼″ (6 mm) of the opposite ends of each piece, and adhere the ends to the back of the coaster, aligned with the ¼″ (6 mm) line **(A)**. Repeat for three more coasters. On the fifth coaster, glue twill to the first and third ⅝″ (1.6 cm) spaces only. Allow the glue to dry completely; erase the pencil marks.

3. With the ⅛″ (3 mm) hole punch or the Japanese screw punch, punch holes in the middle of each piece of twill where it adheres to the coaster. Set eyelets in each hole (see "Twelve-month Organizer, Make the Accordion Bindings" on page 65) **(B)**. Repeat for all coasters.

Bind the Book

1. The book is held together as the cocktail stirrers interlock in the tabs. Insert the first cocktail stirrer through tabs A and C on the cover coaster **(C)**. Insert the second stirrer through tab A on the second coaster, B on the first coaster, C on the second coaster, and D on the first coaster **(D)**. Insert

Ⓐ

Glue twill tapes to coaster.

Ⓑ

Set eyelets through twill tape.

the third stirrer through tab A on the third coaster, B on the second coaster, C on the third coaster, and D on the second coaster. Insert the fourth stirrer through tab A on the fourth coaster, B on the third coaster, C on the fourth coaster, and D on the third coaster. Insert the fifth stirrer though tab A on the fifth coaster, B on the fourth coaster, C on the fifth coaster, and D on the fourth coaster **(E)**.

2. The 3 ½″ x 7″ (8.9 x 17.8 cm) folded pages can be glued to the coasters so they flip up or out to the side. Or adhere 3 ½″ (8.9 cm) squares of cardstock, or leave some coasters as they are. Adhere all extra pages with printed recipes now; the book's ultimate thickness needs to be determined before finishing the binding and closure.

3. Weave a ribbon through the upper and lower ends of the stirrers to add stability to the binding. Cut a 14″ (35.6 cm) piece of the satin ribbon. Place the book fore edge in a vice, between sturdy bookends, or between your knees to hold the pages in place. The spine should be facing up, and the cover facing right. Working around the stirrer lower ends, weave the ribbon from the left under the first stirrer, leaving a 3″ (7.6 cm) tail. Go over the second stirrer, under the third, over the fourth, and under the fifth. Wrap the ribbon around the fifth stirrer, and weave it back to the beginning **(F)**. Tie the ends in a square knot and trim the ends to ¼″ (6 mm). Secure the knot with super glue. Repeat at the opposite ends.

Make the Closure

1. Position the cocktail sword on the cover. Make two marks on either side of the blade just below the handle and about ½″ (1.3 cm) from the tip. With a craft knife, make tiny slits in the coaster to accommodate the ribbons. Cut two 3″ (7.6 cm) pieces of the ribbon and push the ribbon ends through the slits (use the craft knife to carefully push them through). Make sure the ribbons capture the sword, but are not too tight **(G)**. Open the cover, trim the ribbon ends to about ½″ (1.3 cm), and secure with a glue stick.

2. Slip the sword into the ribbons, with the handle facing right. Lace an 8″ (20.3 cm) piece of ribbon through the handle, align the ribbon ends, and bring the ends around to the outside back cover. Mark the back 1 ½″ (3.8 cm) from the fore edge. The ribbon should be tight enough to hold the book closed, but slack enough to remove the sword from the front cover; adjust if necessary. Remove the sword from the front cover. On the back cover mark, cut a small slit to accommodate the ribbons, and push them through **(H)**. Trim the ends to ½″ (1.3 cm), and glue them to the inside back cover. Adhere a single or folded piece of cardstock to the inside front and back covers.

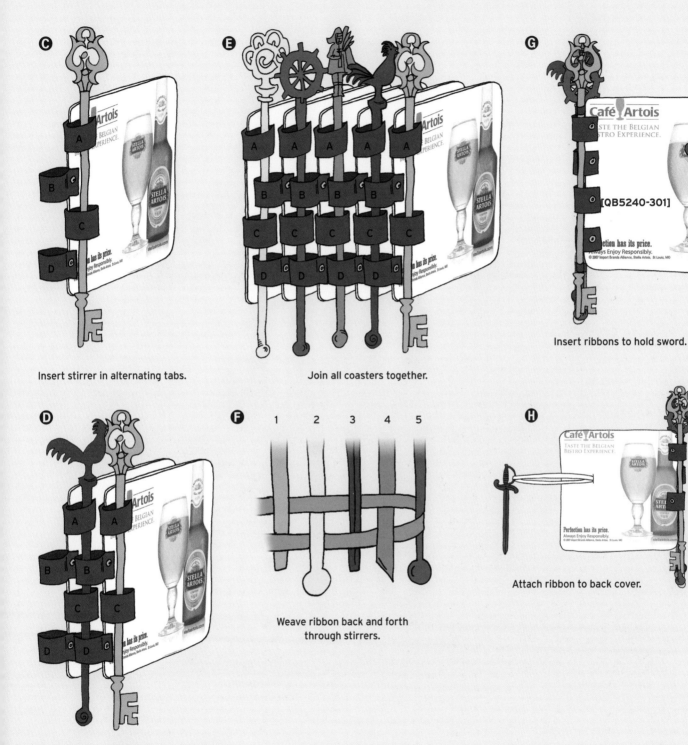

C Insert stirrer in alternating tabs.

E Join all coasters together.

G Insert ribbons to hold sword.

[QB5240-301]

D Insert stirrer in alternating tabs from each coaster.

F Weave ribbon back and forth through stirrers.

H Attach ribbon to back cover.

Pattern-Book Purse Journal

BINDING STYLE: RUNNING STITCH | APPROXIMATE
FINISHED SIZE: 9″ x 7″ (22.9 x 17.8 cm)

What looks like a stylish handbag opens to reveal a take-along journal that's guaranteed to be the envy of every fashionista. Discarded sewing-pattern books form the covers, a handle from a once-loved shoulder bag is shortened and reused, and an old tape measure forms the closures. The hinges are made out of painted and stamped Tyvek, and the signatures are sewn directly to the spine with an easy running stitch. Pages from the pattern book are used as signature wraps, and page tabs are made from clothing labels. The journal opens flat for writing or sketching designs for your next ready-to-wear collection. *Très chic!*

Illustration by Suzi Finer

Materials

- 2 or 3 large sewing-pattern books

- twenty-one 11″ x 7″ (27.9 x 17.8 cm) sheets of card-stock or drawing paper for the text block, grain short, folded in half widthwise (Set aside one folio for signature-punching template. Nest remaining pages into five signatures of four folios each.)

- 5 pages from pattern book for signature wraps, trimmed to 8″ x 7″ (20.3 x 17.8 cm) and folded in half widthwise

- clothing labels

- 8″ x 10″ (20.3 x 25.4 cm) Tyvek rectangle for hinges

- acrylic paint

- paper towels

- rubber stamp

- permanent stamping ink, such as StazOn

- 10″ (25.4 cm) -long handbag strap or belt, approximately ¾″ (1.9 cm) wide (Length may be adjusted longer or shorter.)

- 2 rivets, rivet-setting tools

- five 30″ (76.2 cm) lengths of waxed linen thread

- bookbinding needle

- repositionable low-tack tape

- two 3″ (7.6 cm) lengths cut from ends of tape wmeasure

- two ⅞″ to 1″ (2.2 cm to 2.5 cm) buttons

- extra-sticky adhesive-backed hook-and-loop tape

- PVA

- purse patterns (pages 136, 137, 138)

- spine-punching template (page 138)

- signature-punching guide (page 139)

- sandpaper (optional)

- awl or Japanese screw punch fitted with 1-mm tip

- sewing machine or needle and thread

Prepare the Tyvek Hinges

1. Color the Tyvek with acrylic paint by dabbing a little paint on a paper towel and rubbing it over the Tyvek; repeat until the entire surface is covered; let dry. If desired, decorate the Tyvek with rubber stamps, using permanent ink; let dry. Cut the Tyvek into strips: one 8 ⅞″ x ¾″ (22.5 x 1.9 cm), four 8″ x ¾″ (20.3 x 1.9 cm), and four 10″ x ¾″ (25.4 x 1.9 cm).

Prepare the Covers

1. Copy the patterns on pages 136 to 138, and then cut out the front, back, top, bottom, and flap from the pattern-book covers. (To determine where to cut the cover patterns from the pattern books, see "Tips" on opposite page.)

2. Assemble the purse-cover sections in order, with the outside of the pieces facing up. When hinging the cover sections together, leave a ⅛″ (3 mm) gap between each section to allow them to flex back and forth. (Some pattern books are covered with a plastic coating. If glue has trouble adhering, lightly sand a scant ¼″ [6 mm] along the edge before gluing.) Apply glue to the plain side of the 8″ (20.3 cm) Tyvek strips and join the front flap, top, and back, leaving about ½″

(1.3 cm) overhang at the sides. Use the longest Tyvek strips to join the back, bottom, and front sections, also leaving a ½″ (1.3 cm) overhang **(A)**. Allow all glued Tyvek pieces to dry completely before moving on, pressing the join with weights if necessary. Trim the overhanging ends flush with the cover. Turn the cover over and repeat, making sure the Tyvek strips adhere to each other in the ⅛″ (3 mm) gaps. Fold the remaining Tyvek strip in half lengthwise with the plain sides facing, apply glue to the plain side, and then insert the front-flap edge into the fold. Trim the ends even with the cover.

3. Enlarge the spine-punching template on page 138, cut it out, and then center it on the outside of the bottom panel; secure with repositionable tape. The side where the top of the template is placed will determine which way the pages face when the book is open. For example, with the covers open and the purse handle at the top, placing the top of the template to the right will allow the book to open toward the bottom. Placing it the other way will allow the book to open toward the top. Punch holes with an awl or a Japanese screw punch fitted with the 1-mm tip.

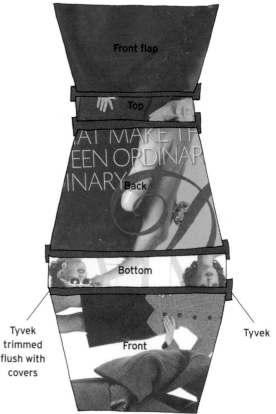

A

Front flap

Top

Back

Bottom

Tyvek trimmed flush with covers

Front

Tyvek

Tyvek strips shown underneath cover pieces to illustrate overlap.

Prepare the Signatures

1. For page tabs attach clothing labels to the page edges with a sewing machine or sew by hand. Cover the fold of each signature with the 8″ x 7″ (20.3 x 17.8 cm) signature wraps. Use the signature-punching guide on page 139 to mark the folio set aside for the signature-punching template. Use the template to punch the signatures.

TRY THIS

- Create covers from promotional signage or record albums.
- Add girly style with marabou, bead trim, or rhinestones.
- Don't toss pattern book pages—use them for decoupage, cards, and envelopes, and in collage projects. Share some with your friends.

Sew the Book

1. All sewing goes through the signatures and the cover. Thread the needle with 30″ (76.2 cm) of waxed linen thread. Pick up the first signature, enter hole #1 from the inside, and secure the 3″ (7.6 cm) tail with repositionable tape. Enter hole #2 from the outside, enter hole #3 from the inside, enter hole #4 from the outside, and enter hole #5 from the inside. Keep the thread taut, pulling it parallel with the spine (B). Sew back up the spine through the same signature: Enter hole #4 from the outside, enter hole #3 from the inside, and enter hole #2 from the outside (C). Do not split the threads when going back though the holes. Pull the thread parallel with the spine to tighten, tie the ends in a square knot inside the signature at hole #1; trim the ends to ¼″ (6 mm). Repeat to sew the remaining signatures to the spine.

Attach the Handle

1. Punch ⅛″ (3 mm) holes ½″ (1.3 cm) from each end of the purse top, centering the holes in the width. Punch ⅛″ (3 mm) holes ⅜″ (1 cm) from each end of the handle. Attach the handle to the purse with rivets following the manufacturer's instructions (D).

Attach the Closures

1. Position the tape-measure pieces 1½″ (3.8 cm) from either side of the front flap, centering the tape on the edge. Sew buttons through the cut ends of the tape-measure pieces onto the front flap, and affix the hook portion of hook-and-loop tape to the opposite ends. Affix the loop portions of the hook-and-loop tape on the purse front (E).

TIPS
- To determine which areas of the pattern-book covers will make an attractive purse, make a viewfinder by tracing the pattern pieces onto cardstock, and then cut out the shape, creating a window. Move the viewfinder around the covers to instantly see which images work best.
- If plastic-coated covers are dirty, clean them with a sparse amount of mild abrasive cleanser (such as Soft Scrub) on a damp paper towel; remove any residue.

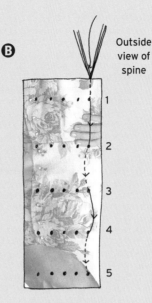

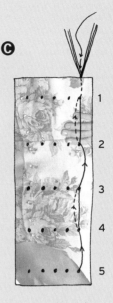

Outside view of spine

Sew down the spine.

Sew back up the spine.

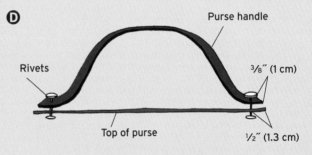

Purse handle

Rivets

⅜″ (1 cm)

Top of purse

½″ (1.3 cm)

Rivets secure handle to purse.

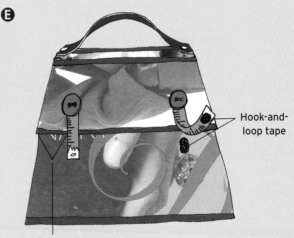

Hook-and-loop tape

1½″ (3.8 cm)

Gallery

A diverse group of artists was asked to interpret the idea of recycling items and materials into books. With few parameters to hinder their creativity, they created an eclectic and stunning array of books that illustrate the exciting possibilities of what can be done with otherwise mundane objects.

Consider this both an art gallery and a launching pad for more ideas, noting that the possibilities for constructing books, journals, photo albums, and scrapbooks using recyclables are endless.

Artist: Marcia Moore, *book artist, teacher, and*
owner of Backspace Book Arts
"Letters/Home" is an artist book constructed of chipboard-
box inserts that have been cut into house shapes, and then
hand painted and letterpress printed. In its embossed cover,
the book lies flat. Once opened, however, it springs to life as
the pages, held together with Coptic stitch, expand into an
entire neighborhood. The book was printed at Shulamis Press
in Venice, California, with the help of Sue Abbe Kaplan.

Artist: Holly Sar Dye, *book artist*

When stacks of expensive, glossy magazines began to crowd her coffee table, Dye took a creative path and turned the pages into a cascading, vibrant concertina with back-to-back folded-and-glued sheets. Ribbon closures accent the elegant style.

Artist: Elaine Nishizu, *book and box artist*

Nishizu's favorite part of eating Cracker Jack was always finding the prize. It was particularly exciting if the prize happened to be a little book. The contents of her "Dream Box" of Cracker Jack is the reverse of what you'd normally find—it's full of miniature books with one piece of caramel popcorn and a peanut. An actual Cracker Jack box and packaging was used for the books and box.

Judi Delgado, *book artist*

This Monopoly-inspired book uses elements from the game to create an accordion structure that fits neatly into a box. The book's pages are property cards, with money sewn into the folds. The box is constructed from the game board, with houses for feet.

Artist: Richard Troncone, *book artist*
In fashioning a book out of items from around his house, Troncone started with an old pair of jeans, cut down to their basic component. Layers of grocery store bags glued together form the cover "boards," lending the book its structure. More grocery store bags are the pages in a traditional, case-bound binding. The denim's origins are revealed in the spine, which features a working zipper.

Artist: Charlene Matthews, *book artist, fine binder and restorer, and owner of Charlene Matthews Bindery*

This recycled travel book, damaged beyond repair, was given a new leather spine and corners. The hollowed-out pages form a cozy niche to store cone-shaped pasties fashioned from the book's pages. The niche is lined with faux suede, and a collage was created using photos from the book.

Artist: Norman Dixon, *paper artist, greeting card designer, and teacher*

Dixon wanted to make a keepsake book to commemorate his fortieth birthday. He used parts of a vintage ledger for the front and back covers, and the birthday cards he received became the inside pages, affixed in a staggered configuration to an accordion fold. The spine is covered with vintage fabric and the cover is embellished with an old photo, plus various salvaged bits. Seam binding acts as a closure.

Artist: Jennifer Kaiser, *book artist*

Soda cans inspired Kaiser to create this book, which uses
flattened cans for pages and tabs for covers. The tabs
were connected by wrapping wire through them to form a
blanket. The pages and covers were sewn together using
wire in a modified Coptic stitch. Wire was wrapped around
and through the can holes, then through the cover. The
straw adds a bit of whimsy.

Artist: Rhonda Miller, *book artist*

This mini library is comprised of five books made from small cereal boxes housed inside a slipcase made from a larger cereal box. Signatures are sewn through the spine, using a basic long stitch. Text pages are various papers salvaged from the recycling bin.

Artist: Andrew Borloz,
owner of Urban Paper Arts,
LLC, providing education,
information, publication, and
design services in the mixed-
media art industry
Borloz created his "Food
Junkie Journal" out of food
packages with colorful,
bold graphics, and bound
it with duct tape, creating
pockets for holding recipe
cards, magazine tear-
sheets, plus menus and
business cards from the
restaurants he frequents.
This hybrid version of a
cookbook, recipe book,
journal, and culinary folder
was inspired by the fact
that Borloz doesn't like
commercial notebooks,
recipe cards, or file folders,
and decided to make his
own.

Artist: Bee Shay, *collage and book artist, printmaker, and teacher*

A recycling center near her home provided Shay with the material for this book. Recycled items have always found their way into her work, providing a challenge to see how those bits and pieces can be reborn for another purpose. Here, covers were constructed from shingles, pages from corrugated cardboard, and the spine from a sweater. Waxed linen thread was used for the through-the-spine binding. Through pictures and text, the book tells the story of the significance of the recycling center in the community.

Artist: Susan Reardon, *book and watercolor artist*

"Neighborhood Gum" celebrates the diverse cultures that combine to become Los Angeles County. The types of gum and their colorful, often innovative wrappings reflect the energy and style of their communities. Materials include corrugated cardboard, gum packages and wrappers, file folders, dressmaker pins, travel brochures, magazine clippings, and images from the Internet. Newspaper ties were used to sew the long-stitch binding.

Artist: Leslie C. Herger,
book artist

A vinyl advertising poster serves as a cover for the larger book, which has inside pockets. Text pages are made from recycled paper. The book was bound with a modified long stitch, using jewelry-maker's hemp. The smaller book is made from a coffee bag, stitched down the spine on a sewing machine using a needle for heavyweight fabrics and cotton quilting thread.

Artist: Dennis Yuen,
book artist, multimedia artist and designer, and partner in Litchinut, a consulting business
Weaving small strips of recycled paper-shopping bags, Yuen created the intricate cover for this oversized book. The woven strips provide a perfect pattern for sewing the long-stitch binding. Inside pages are also created from bags that feature bold colors, familiar logos, and graphics. Yuen is inspired by the physicality of books through interacting with them—holding them, flipping the pages, and touching the bindings.

Artist: Jeannine Stein
After spotting this vintage souvenir wallet at a flea market, I knew it had to be a book. Photos from a recent trip to Europe were incorporated in an accordian pull-out sewn into a fold, and other features were added: metal corners, a button closure, and a book plate. Photographs by Mark Elson.

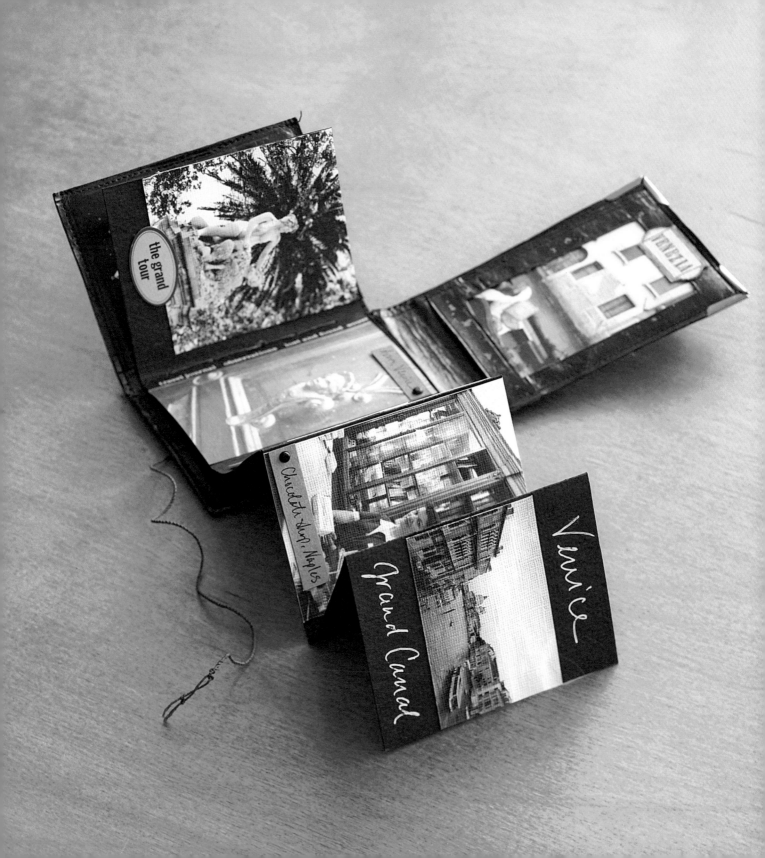

Templates, Patterns, and Guides

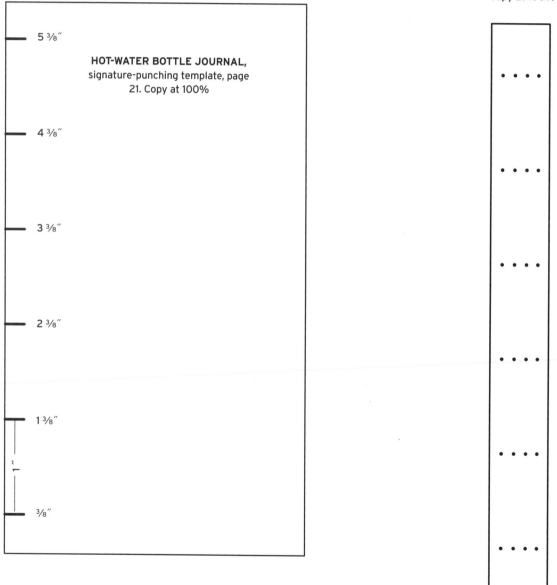

HOT-WATER BOTTLE JOURNAL,
signature-punching template, page
21. Copy at 100%

5 ⅜"

4 ⅜"

3 ⅜"

2 ⅜"

1 ⅜"

1"

⅜"

HOT-WATER BOTTLE JOURNAL,
cover-punching template, page 21.
Copy at 100%

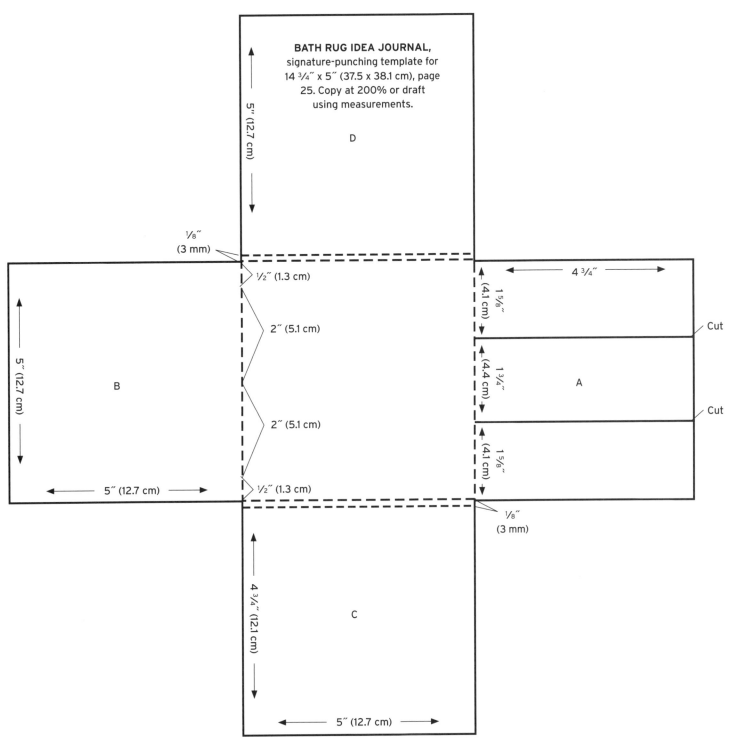

BATH RUG IDEA JOURNAL, signature-punching template for 14 ¾″ x 5″ (37.5 x 38.1 cm), page 25. Copy at 200% or draft using measurements.

D

5″ (12.7 cm)

⅛″ (3 mm)

½″ (1.3 cm)

2″ (5.1 cm)

2″ (5.1 cm)

½″ (1.3 cm)

B

5″ (12.7 cm)

5″ (12.7 cm)

4 ¾″

1 ⅝″ (4.1 cm)

Cut

1 ¾″ (4.4 cm)

A

Cut

1 ⅝″ (4.1 cm)

⅛″ (3 mm)

C

4 ¾″ (12.1 cm)

5″ (12.7 cm)

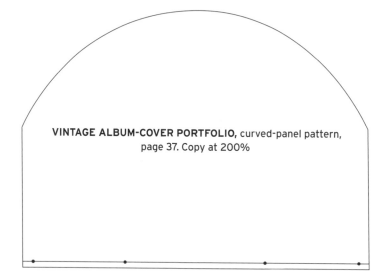

VINTAGE ALBUM-COVER PORTFOLIO, curved-panel pattern, page 37. Copy at 200%

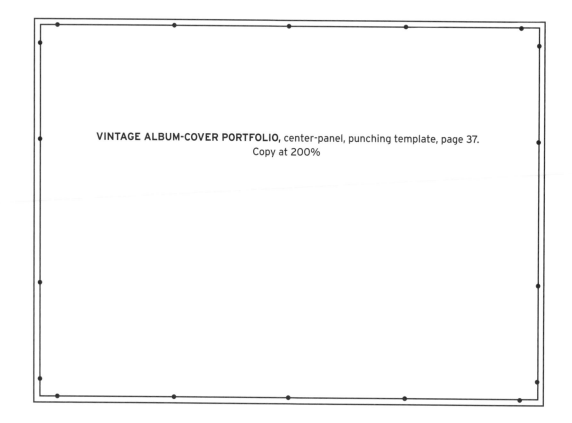

VINTAGE ALBUM-COVER PORTFOLIO, center-panel, punching template, page 37. Copy at 200%

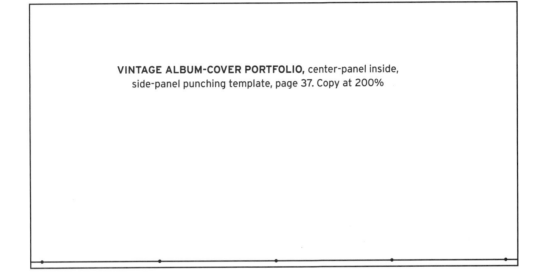

VINTAGE ALBUM-COVER PORTFOLIO, center-panel inside,
side-panel punching template, page 37. Copy at 200%

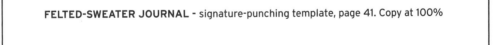

FELTED-SWEATER JOURNAL - signature-punching template, page 41. Copy at 100%

FELTED SWEATER JOURNAL, cover-punching template, page 41. Copy at 100%

CABINET-CARD SKETCHBOOK, signature-punching template, page 45.
Copy at 100%

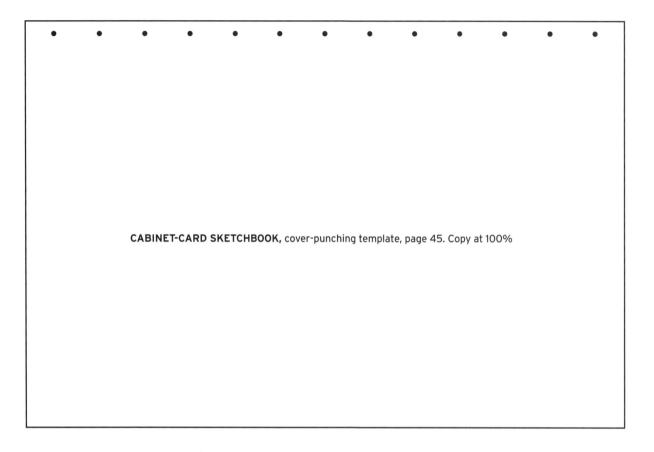

CABINET-CARD SKETCHBOOK, cover-punching template, page 45. Copy at 100%

CABINET-CARD SKETCHBOOK, spine-punching template, page 45. Copy at 100%

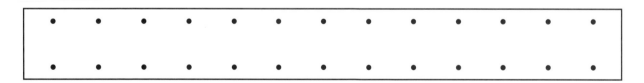

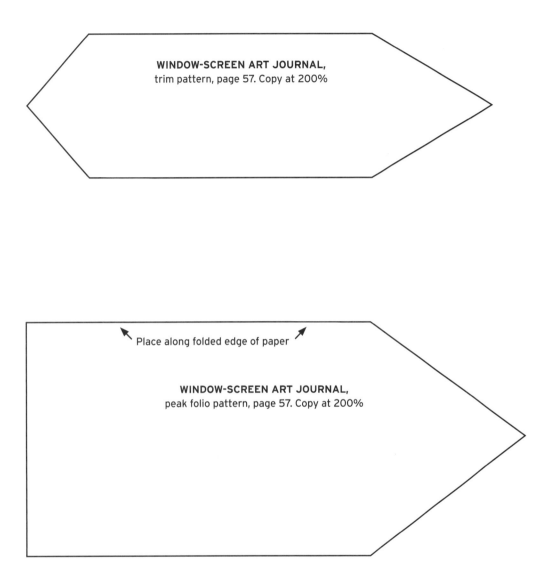

WINDOW-SCREEN ART JOURNAL,
trim pattern, page 57. Copy at 200%

Place along folded edge of paper

WINDOW-SCREEN ART JOURNAL,
peak folio pattern, page 57. Copy at 200%

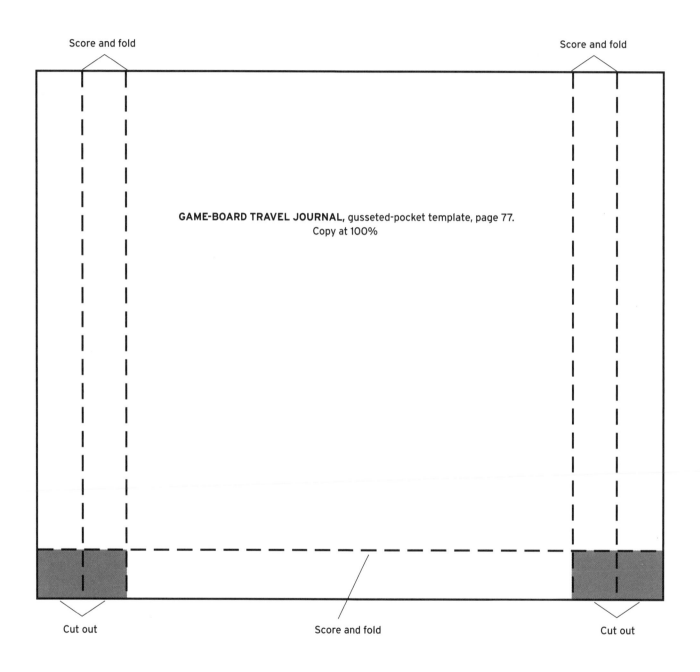

Score and fold

Score and fold

GAME-BOARD TRAVEL JOURNAL, gusseted-pocket template, page 77.
Copy at 100%

Cut out

Score and fold

Cut out

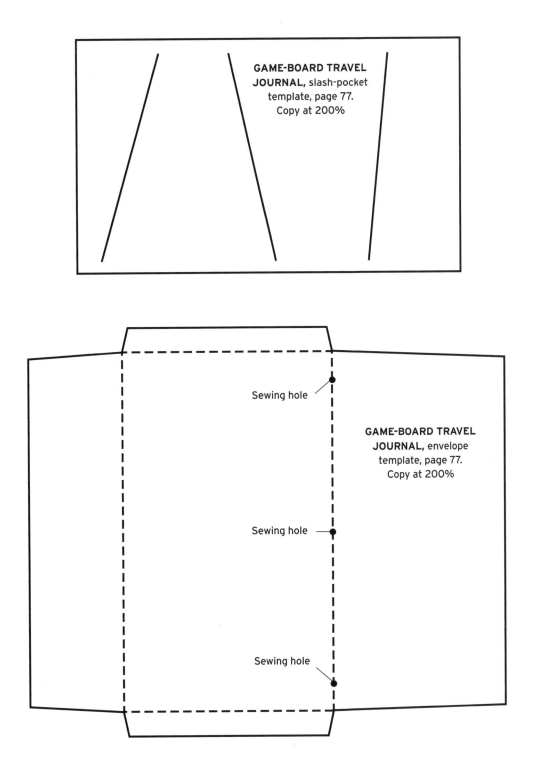

GAME-BOARD TRAVEL JOURNAL, slash-pocket template, page 77. Copy at 200%

GAME-BOARD TRAVEL JOURNAL, envelope template, page 77. Copy at 200%

Sewing hole

Sewing hole

Sewing hole

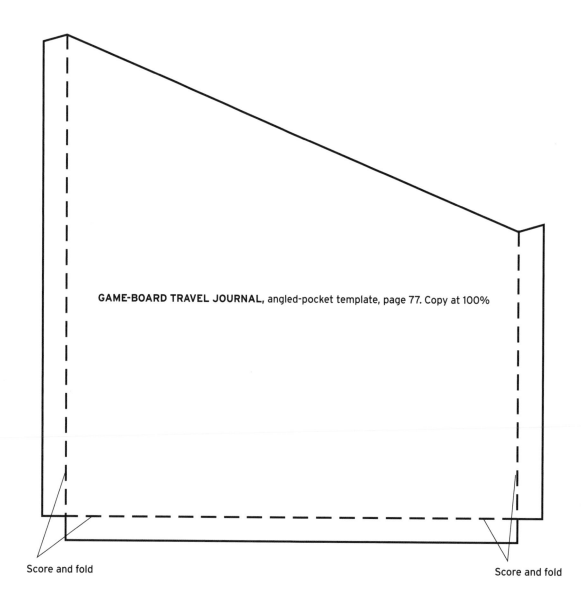

GAME-BOARD TRAVEL JOURNAL, angled-pocket template, page 77. Copy at 100%

Score and fold

Score and fold

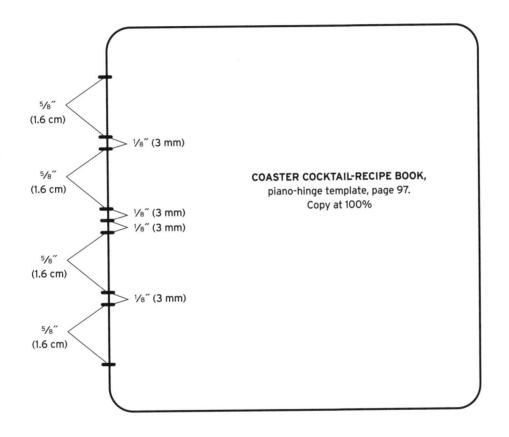

⁵⁄₈″ (1.6 cm)

¹⁄₈″ (3 mm)

⁵⁄₈″ (1.6 cm)

¹⁄₈″ (3 mm)

¹⁄₈″ (3 mm)

⁵⁄₈″ (1.6 cm)

¹⁄₈″ (3 mm)

⁵⁄₈″ (1.6 cm)

COASTER COCKTAIL-RECIPE BOOK,
piano-hinge template, page 97.
Copy at 100%

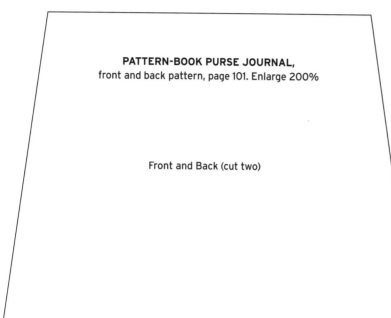

PATTERN-BOOK PURSE JOURNAL,
front and back pattern, page 101. Enlarge 200%

Front and Back (cut two)

Top

PATTERN-BOOK PURSE JOURNAL, top pattern, page 101. Copy at 100%

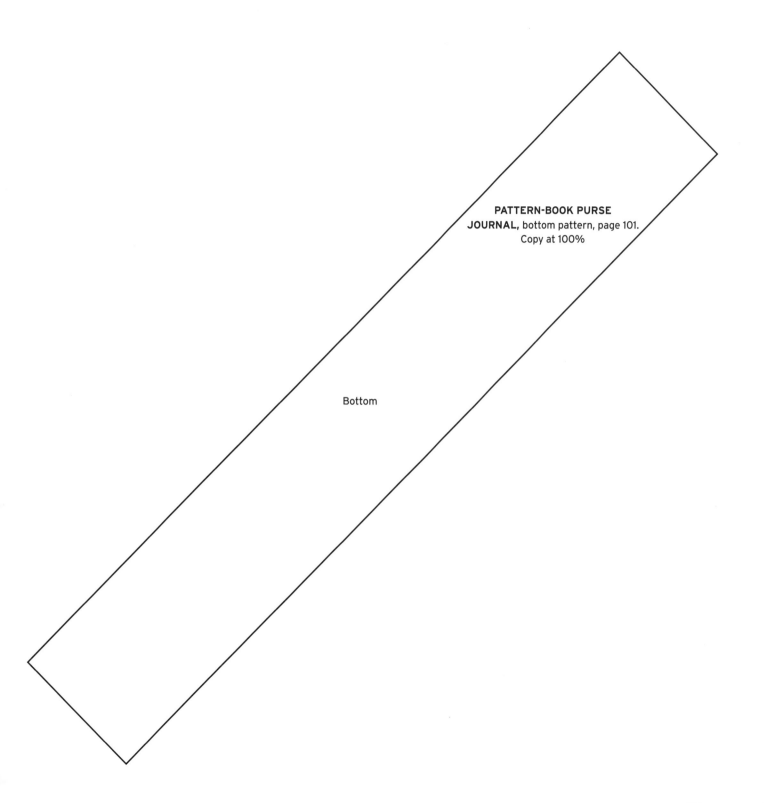

PATTERN-BOOK PURSE
JOURNAL, bottom pattern, page 101.
Copy at 100%

Bottom

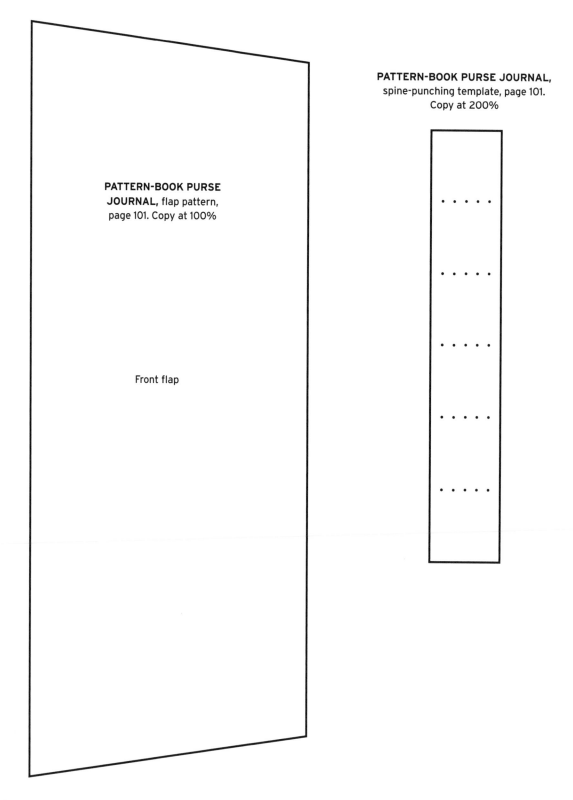

PATTERN-BOOK PURSE JOURNAL, flap pattern, page 101. Copy at 100%

Front flap

PATTERN-BOOK PURSE JOURNAL, spine-punching template, page 101. Copy at 200%

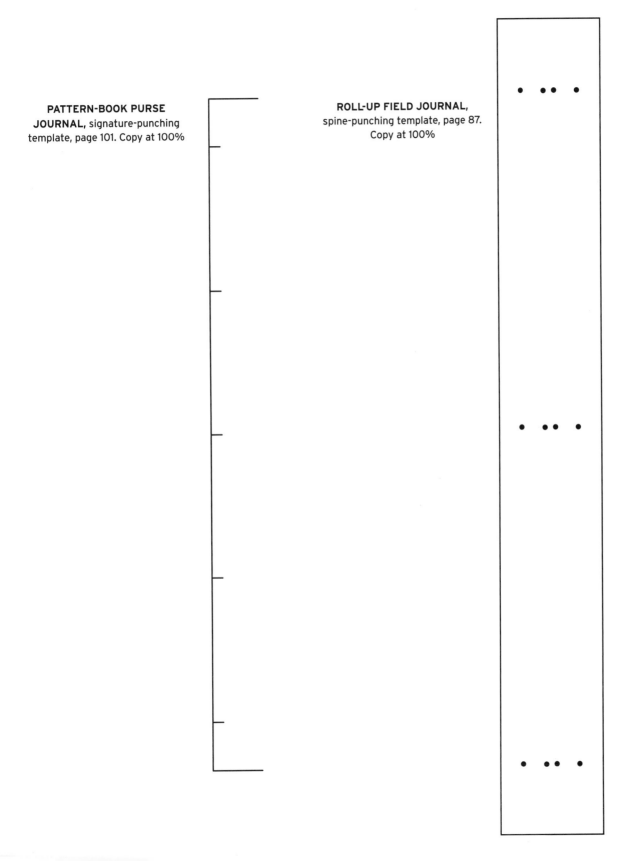

PATTERN-BOOK PURSE JOURNAL, signature-punching template, page 101. Copy at 100%

ROLL-UP FIELD JOURNAL, spine-punching template, page 87. Copy at 100%

Contributors

Andrew Borloz
Urban Paper Arts, LLC
andrew@urbanpaperarts.com
www.urbanpaperarts.com

Judi Delgado
delgadojx@yahoo.com

Norman Dixon
normanpdixon@hotmail.com
www.normandixon.etsy.com

Holly Sar Dye
hsd@bufobufo.com
www.hollydye.typepad.com

Leslie C. Herger
Comfortable Shoes Studio
Leslie.Herger@gmail.com
www.comfortableshoesstudio.com

Jennifer Kaiser
Deckled Edge Bindery
decklededgebindery@yahoo.com
www.decklededgebindery.etsy.com

Charlene Matthews
Charlene Matthews Bindery
bindery@sbcglobal.net
www.charlenematthews.com

Rhonda Miller
pertelote@ns.sympatico.ca
www.myhandboundbooks.com
www.myhandboundbooks.etsy.com

Marcia Moore
Backspace Book Arts
marcia@backspacebookarts.com
www.backspacebookarts.com

Elaine Nishizu
enishizu@gmail.com

Susan Reardon
smreardon@worldnet.att.net

Bee Shay
Heart 2 Hand Studio
bee.shay@hotmail.com
www.beeshay.typepad.com

Richard Troncone
richtroncone@yahoo.com
www.richtroncone.com

Dennis Yuen
dennis@studiocailun.com
www.studiocailun.com

Stitch Glossary

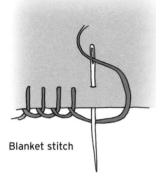

Blanket stitch

Slipknot

Square knot

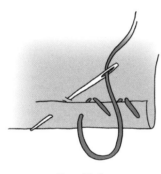

Hemstitch

Single knot

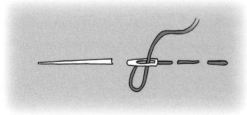

Running stitch

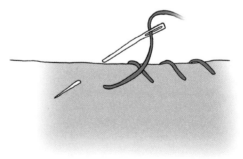

Whip stitch

Supplies and Resources

Book Arts Guilds, Resources, and Forums

The Bookarts Forum
www.bookartsforum.com

The Book Arts Web
www.philobiblon.com

Guild of Book Workers
521 5th Ave.
New York, NY 10175
USA
www.palimpsest.stanford.edu/byorg/gbw
communications@guildofbookworkers.allmail.net

Bookbinding Supplies

Bookmakers International
8601 Rhode Island Ave.
College Park, MD 20740
USA
301.345.7979
www.bookmakerscatalog.com
bookmakers@earthlink.net

Dick Blick Art Materials
P.O. Box 1267
Galesburg, IL 61402
USA
800.933.2542
www.dickblick.com
info@dickblick.com

Hollanders
410 N. 4th Ave.
Ann Arbor, MI 48104
USA
734.741.7531
www.hollanders.com
info@hollanders.com

John Neal Bookseller
1833 Spring Garden St.
Greensboro, NC 27403
USA
800.369.9598
www.johnnealbooks.com
info@johnnealbooks.com

Paper Source
410 N. Milwaukee Ave.
Chicago, IL 60654
USA
888.727.3711
www.paper-source.com
customerservice@paper-source.com

Talas
20 W. 20th St., 5th Floor
New York, NY 10011
USA
212.219.0770
www.talasonline.com
info@talasonline.com

Tyvek
Recycled overnight envelopes, such as FedEx; also available new in office supply stores

Classes in Bookbinding and Book Arts

The Center for Book Arts
28 W. 27th St., 3rd Floor
New York, NY 10001
USA
212.481.0295
www.centerforbookarts.org
info@centerforbookarts.org

Minnesota Center for Book Arts
1011 Washington Ave. S., Ste. 100
Minneapolis, MN 55415
USA
612.215.2520
www.mnbookarts.org
mcba@mnbookarts.org

Penland School of Crafts
P.O. Box 37
Penland, NC 28765
USA
828.765.2359
www.penland.org
info@penland.org

San Diego Book Arts
www.sandiegobookarts.org
San Francisco Center for the Book
300 De Haro St.
San Francisco, CA 94103
USA
415.565.0545
www.sfcb.org

Free Recycled Materials

Craigslist
www.craigslist.org

The Freecycle Network
P.O. Box 294
Tucson, AZ 85702
USA
www.freecycle.org
info@freecycle.org

Vintage Items Online

Collage Stuff
www.collagestuff.com
thelisalisa@collagestuff.com

Ebay
www.ebay.com

Etsy
www.etsy.com

Papier Valise
403.277.1802
www.papiervalise.com
janice@papervalise.com

Vintage Charmings
www.vintagecharmings.com

About the Author

Jeannine Stein has been making handmade books for more than fifteen years, exploring bindings, mediums, and materials. Her work has been featured in other Quarry books such as *Pockets, Pullouts, and Hiding Places*, *Beyond Scrapbooks*, and *100 Ideas for Stationery, Cards, and Invitations*, as well as national magazines.

She has been teaching book arts for several years, and her commissioned work includes wedding albums, guest books, photo albums, and journals.

Jeannine is a journalist living in Los Angeles with her husband Mark Elson, a photographer and filmmaker.

Acknowledgments

A great amount of thanks go to my family and friends, who provided wonderful support and feedback before and during the writing of this book.

A huge thank-you to my editor, Mary Ann Hall, for her guidance, unwavering good judgment, and encouragement, and to Quarry Books for giving me this opportunity. I am truly grateful.

Gratitude goes to the amazing teachers I've had over the years, who inspired me, bestowed confidence, and showed patience. Your influence flows throughout this book.

To the incredible artists who contributed to this book, thank you for your talent and time, and for the delight in opening the boxes that held your beautiful creations.

And of course, thank you to my husband Mark, the love of my life, whose help and support was immeasurable. Thanks for putting up with the mess. I promise I'll clean it up.

Jeannine Stein can be reached at jsteinelson@yahoo.com.